al-G...
Jewels of the Quran

(Jawāhir al-Qur'ān)

Abū Ḥāmid Muḥammad al-Ghazzālī Ṭūsī

EDITED BY

LALEH BAKHTIAR

SERIES EDITOR
SEYYED HOSSEIN NASR

GREAT BOOKS OF THE ISLAMIC WORLD

2 *Jewels of the Quran*

© Laleh Bakhtiar 2009

Library of Congress Cataloging-in-Publication Data

Jewels of the Quran. English. Edited by Laleh Bakhtiar

I. Bakhtiar, Laleh. II. Title

BP130.4.G4513   297'.1226   83-17533

ISBN: 1567447600

Published by
Great Books of the Islamic World

Distributed by
Kazi Publications, Inc
3023 West Belmont Avenue
Chicago IL 60618

Contents

Editor's Preface

Working in a Muslim publishing house like Kazi Publications, Inc., for over fifteen years, I am continuously meeting new manuscripts, new ways of expressing the various aspects of Islamic culture and civilization. One of the most interesting encounters took place a year ago after the translation of the *Sublime Quran* was published.

Two manuscripts were sent—translations of Abu Hamid Muhammad al-Ghazzali—*Jewels of the Quran* and a translation of a part of *Revival of the Religious Sciences* dealing with the recitation and interpretation of the Quran.

The person who sent them asked to remain anonymous as his field of expertise is in an area other than that of the Quran. He said once he read the English translation of the *Sublime Quran*, he thought of these two books, how a translation and publication of them using the signs or verses from the *Sublime Quran* would greatly enhance the reader's experience of both.

It was with great anticipation that I read the translations. The works of Abu Hamid al-Ghazzali never cease to amaze me. While most subject indices of the Quran focus on the external or outward meaning, al-Ghazzali's selection in *Jewels of the Quran* of over 1500 signs from the Quran concentrate on how to apply the signs to our personal development.

After an introduction of nineteen short chapters, he divides the signs of the Quran into two types which he calls Rubies and Pearls. The 763 Ruby signs help the reader to gain knowledge of God's essence, His names and qualities and His acts. As he has selected these signs to follow one another, the reader encounters a concentration of this form of theoretical knowledge.

Then he turns our attention to the 741 Pearl signs that show the reader the various aspects of the straight path.

These are the practical aspects of the signs. They point Muslims to what they need to be putting into practice in order to be able to claim that they follow the straight path.

Al-Ghazzali's creative approach to the signs of the Quran will give the reader a completely different experience than simply using them as a reference for various topics.

It did not take any convincing on my part for Liaquat Ali, President of Kazi Publications, Inc. to agree to publish them if I edited them and added my translation of the Quran to al-Ghazzali's references to the Quranic signs. This I have done.

May God forgive any errors I may have made as the responsibility for them are my own.

Laleh Bakhtiar, Ph. D.
Chicago, 2009

In the Name of God, The Merciful, The Compassionate.

Author's Foreword

All praise belongs to God alone, the Lord of all worlds. May his blessing be on His Prophet Muhammad, on all his family and all his companions.

Know, may God guide you to his path that we have arranged this book in four parts:

Part 1: Introduction
Part 2: The Rubies of the Quran
Part 3: The Pearls of the Quran
Part 4: Conclusion

The Introduction consists of nineteen chapters:

Chapter 1: On how the Quran is like an ocean that contains all kinds of jewels and precious gems

Chapter 2: On dividing the principles of the Quran and its precious gems into six categories. Three are the main categories containing the principles and three are sub-categories, completing them.

Chapter 3: On the explanation of the six categories that branch out to make ten topics

Chapter 4: On how all knowledge branches off from these ten topics and how the knowledge of the Quran is divided into knowledge of the outer shells and knowledge of the inner jewels and a description of different types of knowledge

Chapter 5: On how previous and present types of knowledge branch off from the Quran

Chapter 6: On the meaning of the statement that the Quran contains red sulfur, the greatest antidote, the most aromatic musk and all other kinds of precious gems including rubies and pearls. This is only perceived by those who know the relationship between the manifest and the hidden worlds.

Chapter 7: On the reasons why the entities of the hidden world are explained in the Quran using examples from the manifest world

Chapter 8: On comprehending the relationship between the manifest and hidden worlds

Chapter 9: On the description of the symbols underlying red sulfur, the greatest antidote, the most aromatic musk, pearls and so on

Chapter 10: On the benefits of using these signs

Chapter 11: On the excellence of some signs of the Quran more than others when they are all the Word of God

Chapter 12: On the mysteries of the Opening Chapter and how it contains eight of the ten kinds of precious gems of the Quran and the description of part of the meaning of The Merciful, the Compassionate in relationship to the nature of animals

Chapter 13: On the eight doors to the Garden and how they are opened through the Opening Chapter and that it has the keys to all of them

Chapter 14: On why the sign of the "Throne" (2:255) is regarded as the major sign of the Quran and why this is so rather than 3:18, 112:1, 57:1-6, 59:22-24 and all other signs

Chapter 15: On why the Chapter on Sincere Expression (112) is valued as a third of the Quran

Chapter 16: On why Chapter Ya Sin (36) is regarded as the heart of the Quran

Chapter 17: On why the Prophet specified the Opening Chapter as the best Chapter of the Quran and the sign of the "Throne" as the major sign of the Quran and the reason why this sign was better than its opposites

Chapter 18: On the condition of the knowers (gnostics) in this world

Chapter 19: On the reason for separating the rubies from the pearls in the Quran

These are the 19 Chapters in Part 1: Introduction

Part 2: The Rubies of the Quran

The rubies of the Quran are signs that refer to the divine Essence, the divine names and qualities and divine acts. This is the knowledge base.

Part 3: The Pearls of the Quran

The Pearls of the Quran on the signs that describe the straight path and signs that encourage the human being to follow the straight path. This is the practical base.

Part 4: Conclusion

Why the discussion of the Quranic signs has been confined to the categories of rubies and pearls* (*Following this al-Ghazzali describes the forty parts of his work *Kitab al-arba'īn fī uṣūl al-dīn* (The Book of the Forty on the Principles of the Way of Life).

Part 1: Introduction
Chapter 1: On how the Quran is like an ocean that contains all kinds of jewels and precious gems

In the Name of God, The Merciful, The Compassionate.

After mentioning the name of God, I glorify Him and praise Him. Every book should begin in this way. May His blessings be upon His Messengers! This is a supplication by which every book should end.

I hope to awaken you from your sleep, O you who recite a lengthy portion of the Quran, you who take study it as an occupation and who glean some of its manifest meanings. How long will you be content with just these meanings of the Quran?

Do you not have a duty to sail into the endless ocean of its meanings? Are you not to arrive at the best understanding? Dive into the ocean's depths so that you become wealthy by gaining its rubies and pearls. Why do you persist in remaining on the shore, satisfied with the manifest.

Do you not know that the Quran is like an ocean. Knowledge of the previous and present scholars branch off from the Quran much like rivers and streams branch off from the shores of an ocean.

Why is it that you chose not to follow the way of those people? They courageously overcame the waves of the ocean. It was in this way that they gained rubies and pearls. They journeyed along the coasts to gather grey ambergris and aloeswood. They were attracted to the islands. They found the greatest antidote and most aromatic musk from the animals there. In fulfilling my duty of brotherhood and hoping for the blessings of your supplication, I now guide you to the journey of these people, of their diving into the vast ocean of the Quran and swimming in it in an effort to fulfill my duty of brotherhood and in the hope for blessings from your supplications.

Chapter 2: On dividing the principles of the Quran and its precious gems into six categories: Three are the main categories containing the principles and three are sub-categories completing them.

The mystery of the Quran, its essence and ultimate purpose is to invite "the servants of God," to "*the Powerful, the Lord of this present life and the world to come*" (53:25), "*the Creator of the lofty heavens, the earth below, and whatever is in and on the earth*" (20:6).

The chapters and signs of the Quran have been divided into six categories. Three categories are the main ones containing the principles. And the other three types are sub-categories and completing the first three:

The first three main categories describe the principles as follows:

The first main category is the description of God, the One to Whom you are being called. The second main category is the description of the straight path (1:6) that should be adhered to in reaching toward Him. The third main category is the description of the state upon reaching Him.

The three sub-categories that complete the categories are the following.

The first sub-category describes those who respond to the call to God, how He deals gently with them, the mystery and aim of this being to awaken a desire in people and encourage them in this way. It also describes the state of those who refuse to respond to the invitation. It includes the way that God will punish them, the aim of this being to instigate awareness and Godfearingness.

The second sub-category recounts the states of those who are ungrateful to God, revealing their scandals and state of ignorance in argument and contesting against The Truth. By highlighting falsehood, God intends to discredit it and by highlighting The Truth, to deepen awareness of it.

The third supplementary category recounts the stations on the way to nearness to God and the means by which provision would be made available and readiness for it would be shown.

Chapter 3: On the explanation of the six categories that branch out to make ten topics

The first of the categories of the Quran define God, the One to Whom human beings are called. It is to explain knowledge of God. Knowledge of the divine essence is called red sulfur. This knowledge includes knowledge of the divine essence, knowledge of the divine names and qualities and knowledge of the divine acts. These three are referred to as the ruby, purplish blue sapphire and yellow sapphire respectively as these are the most significant precious gems derived from red sulfur.

The foregoing three categories of knowledge may be likened to red, purplish blue and yellow gems which develop from the main benefits of red sulfur. Some of these gems are more difficult to come by, more precious than others.

In the same way, these three forms of knowledge are not of the same rank but are classified according to preciousness. The most precious is the first, knowledge of God's divine essence. Therefore this should be called the ruby. The second is knowledge of the divine names and qualities. This is the purplish blue sapphire. Along with this knowledge is knowledge of the divine acts. This would be the yellow sapphire.

The ruby is that which is the most rare and the most difficult to mine to the extent that even monarchs and sultans do not usually manage to obtain but a very little quantity. They might even fail to obtain but far less quality. In the same way knowledge of the divine essence is the most restricted knowledge, the hardest to obtain, the most difficult to comprehend, and the furthest from all other types of knowledge. This is the reason why the Quran only contains intimations of this knowledge. Expressions of it are very succinct like the Word of God: *"There is not like Him anything"* (42:11); *"there is nothing comparable to Him"* (112:4); *"glory be to Him! Exalted is He above what they allege. He is the Beginner of the heavens and the earth."* (6:100-101)

As for the divine names and qualities, the description of these is greater. Most of the signs of the Quran referring to the divine names and qualities refer aspects of divine knowledge, power, life, speech, wisdom, hearing and seeing.

As for divine acts, they are comparable to an ocean that has extensive shores, the extent of which are difficult to come by. As a matter of fact, nothing exists other than through His acts. Everything that exists are His acts.

The Quran mentions the clearly observable of them, that which exists in the manifest world such as the heavens, the planets, the earth, mountains, trees, animals, seas, plants, sending down of sweet water and all other means of sustaining plants and life. These are the divine acts that are clearly observable to the senses.

Yet the most splendid, honorable and glorious manifestations are those hidden to our senses, originated by the Creator. These are but divine Self-disclosures, angelic and spiritual, as well as that of the soul and spiritual heart, that is the aspects of the human being that know God. They are beyond sense perception.

The divine acts also include the terrestrial angels entrusted with the care of the human being. It was these angels who prostrated to Adam. Among the others are the satans who whisper to human beings. It is they who refrained from prostrating to Adam when so commanded by God. Then there are the celestial angels, the highest of whom in degree are the archangels. They are hidden in the Garden, paying no attention to the human being at all. They attend not to anything other than God. They are absorbed in the beauty of His glory. They gaze at Him alone, glorifying Him day and night without every tiring. *"They glorify Him nighttime and daytime. They never decrease."* (21:20)

It is no surprise that some of God's servants contemplate and ponder more about the beauty and glory of God than anything else, even more than Adam and his offspring. Yet nothing of this could exalt the human being to the state of the Messenger of God who said: Verily God extends a vast and expanse of white land where the sun could roam in thirty days thirty times of our worldly days, replete with human beings who have no idea about the fact that God is being disobeyed and have no idea that God had created Adam and Satan. (Related by Ibn Abbas).

Thus we find that God's kingdom expands beyond the limits of the human mind.

Let it be known too that most of humanity literally ignores the most honorable acts of God. Yet more than this they stand unable to recognize those acts. This is because they are accustomed to observable objects. These are but the superficial results of the sovereignty that lies far from the divine essence. Whoever does not step beyond this threshold would then be more like one who just saw the skin of a pomegranate without digging deeper to the seeds. From amongst the wonders of the human being, they would only see their complexion.

This was the first section whereby you would be cognizant of the categories of knowledge. We will provide you with the signs recited from the Quran in this regard which are deemed to be the essence, heart and mystery of the Quran.

The second main category relates to a description of the straight path, "*the path of those to whom Thou hast been gracious*" (1:6) that should be adhered to reach the target of the message of God. One can get to know the path to God through devotion as said by God: "*And remember the Name of thy Lord and devote thyself to Him with total devotion*" (73:8) namely, one should seek God's satisfaction by approaching God and staying far from sin and whichever aspect that would cause God's wrath be poured upon oneself. This would by all means be materialized in the sign "*The Lord of the East and the West, there is no God but He.*" (73:9)

Approaching God can only be attained by purifying oneself from the affairs and troubles of this present world, by purifying the soul from them. The end result of this would be one's leaning toward the world to come as God said: "*He certainly prospered, he who purified himself.*" (87:14-15) This way relies on two issues: Obedience and disobedience. That is, obedience in observing one's duty to God and disobedience to whatever takes one away from Him and His remembrance. This is the journey to God.

On this journey to God there is no movement from the one who is journeying nor from Him toward Whom he journeys as both are already together. As the Quran says: "*We are nearer to him than the jugular vein.*" (50:16).

Compare the seeker and the Sought to an image in a mirror: A rusty mirror will not reflect an image. However, when the rust is removed and the mirror polished, an image can appear in it, not by any movement of the image towards it nor by its movement towards the image. The image is now apparent because of the removal of that which had veiled it.

Then and only then would God be manifested clearly without any obstruction in such a way that no other object would preclude Him from His Self-disclosure. This is because His light is an eternal light. Nothing in the universe can prevent it from shinning. With such Self-disclosure, each and every hidden object would come to light, humbled. This is because God is the light of the heavens and the earth: *"God is the Light of the heavens and the earth. The parable of His Light is as a niche in which there is a lamp. The lamp is in a glass. The glass is as if it had been a glittering star, kindled from the blessed olive tree, neither eastern nor western, whose oil is about to illuminate although no fire touches it. Light on light, God guides to His Light whom He wills! And God propounds parables for humanity, and God is Knowing of everything."* (24:35)

The light is concealed from the human eye for two reasons: Either because of a defect in the pupil of the eye that then renders the light unable to be seen clearly or by weakness in the pupil so that it is not able to bear the glorious and magnificent light as bats are unable to bear the light of the sun. Therefore the only thing one must do is to cleanse one's heart from its blemishes and the eye from its defect. Then one would be able to see the light clearly. The image would show itself in the mirror.

Then it will appear as if God is in the soul as the image in the mirror. When He suddenly Self-discloses in the mirror of the soul, you are quick to say that He is on the inside of the soul itself and that human nature has taken on the divine nature. Then you persevere until God enhances you with the Firm Word: *"God makes firm those who have believed with the firm saying in this present life and in the world to come and God will cause to go astray the ones who are unjust. And God accomplishes what He wills,"* (14:27) so that you come to know that the image is not really inside the mirror, but only reflected in it.

If the image were to be actually inside the mirror, it would not be possible for it to reflect on many mirrors at one and the same time. Instead it would be that when it is inside one mirror, it has moved there from another mirror. This, however, is not the case because God Self-discloses to many of the knowers (gnostics) at one and the same time. He Self-discloses to some mirrors of the soul more completely, in a more direct and clearer manner, and to others more mysteriously and indirectly. This difference is because the mirror has become clear of rust, polished, perfected in shape and correct in the width of its surface. This is why the Prophet said: God Self-disclosed to the people in general and to Abu Bakr in particular.

Knowing how to advance towards God on the straight path and how to attain to Him is like the profound ocean from the oceans of the Quran. The signs are to guide you to the straight path so that you are able to contemplate all together and so that you might unravel everything surrounding you. This is the aspect of the Quranic signs that form brilliant pearls.

The third main category describes the human being's state at the time of drawing near to Him. It narrates the rest and the happiness he will attain. The all-encompassing term to describe all types of rest and peace is the Garden. The highest Garden is the pleasure of looking upon God. The Quran also mentions the humiliation and the punishment that will be borne by those who are veiled from Him because of their not choosing to travel the path to Him. The all-encompassing term to describe all types of pain and suffering is hell. The most extreme form of pain refers to that borne by those who are veiled from Him, at a distance from Him. This is why He mentioned in the Quran: *"No indeed! They will be from their Lord on that Day ones who are alienated."* (83:15)

The third main category refers to both the people of the Garden and the people of hell. Their situation is explained through concepts like the resurrection, raising the dead, guarding and reckoning, the balance, and the bridge. There are clear manifest meanings to these, as well, which act as food for the common person. But the words also have special symbolic meanings for those who are special.

The third category of the signs of the Quran concern details about these subjects. They will not be presented here in this book because they are too numerous. One can reflect on them and search for them. The third main category is the green emerald.

The fourth main category of the Quran consists of the situation of those who have journeyed on the path to God and those who deny Him and deviate from His way. Those who have journeyed on the path to God are mentioned in the stories of the prophets and angels: Adam, Noah, Abraham, Moses, Aaron, Zachariah, John, Jesus, Mary, David, Solomon, Jonah, Lot, Enoch, Khidr, Shuayb, Elias, Muhammad, Gabriel, Michael, and other angels, and so on, peace be upon them all.

The situation of those who have denied Him and have deviated from His way are the stories of Nimrod, Pharaoh, Ad, the people of Lot, the Companions of the Wood, the ungrateful of Mecca, those who worship idols, the satans, and so on. This division is to create fear, to give warning. They are put forward as things to consider. It also includes intimations which require much reflection. Grey ambergris and aloeswood are found in describing the situations of these two groups. There are too many signs concerning them to make gathering them useful.

The fifth main category of the Quranic signs relates to the arguments of the ungrateful against The Truth. The arguments are clear and distinct explanations of how humiliating their arguments are. This is shown through clear proofs, the disclosure of their falsity and self-deceit. Their falsity consists of three kinds: The first is in speaking of God in terms that are not respectful of Him such as where they say that the angels are daughters of God; that he had a child, that He has associates and partners, and that He is "the third of three."

The second is to take into account those signs that indicate that the Messenger of God was a sorcerer or a madman or a liar, to deny his prophethood and to claim that he does not need to be followed because he is a man like other men.

The third section relates to those who deny the Last Day, the resurrection, the raising of the dead, the Garden, hell and the refusal to believe in the recompense for obedience or disobedience to God. The Quran gives arguments with proof against those who are ungrateful. An important antidote is contained in the hidden and the manifest meanings of these signs. However they are also too numerous to gather together.

The sixth main category of Quranic signs clarifies how one is to fulfill one's obligations on the various stations of the path to God. They show what provisions are necessary and how to be prepared for the journey by preparing the weapons which will hold off the thieves along the way. This can be explained by saying that the world is one of the stations along the way for those who journey to God. Their body is their means of transportation. The person who disregards this station and the means of transportation will not be able to reach the end of the journey.

A person who wishes to undertake this journey but first must set his affairs in order, especially that of his livelihood. Without this, a person will be denied the ability to be completely devoted to God which is the same as undertaking the journey to God. That devotion also requires that one's body be sound and his children cared for. This is attained by preserving their existence and repelling whatever corrupts and destroys them. In order to preserve their existence, they must eat and drink, meet their physical needs, in addition to engaging in sexual intercourse in order to reproduce.

Food is that which sustains life and females are a means for the species to continue.

However, some people do not require food and women because of their innate nature. If these issues were left undecided, without a legal definition, people would have fought one another instead of treading the right path. The fighting would have caused such strive for them that they would not have followed the straight path that leads to a righteous end.

As a result, the Quran has explained the laws in regard to wealth through the signs dealing with transactions, usury, giving and receiving loans, division of inheritance, the necessary expenditures, how to divide up spoils of war, giving of charity, marriage, the freeing of slaves through buying oneself freedom, having slaves and prisoners of war. The Quran also describes the manner of gaining wealth including taking oaths and having witnesses.

In regard to women, the Quran mentions signs related to marriage, divorce, not divorcing, laws regarding widows or divorced women before they may remarry, divorce initiated by a woman, dowry, divorce where a husband declares not to have sexual intercourse with his wife for not less than four months, the issues that arise when a husband declares "be as my mother's back," a divorce that takes place after a husband accuses his wife of adultery and each of them swear an oath to God that each one of them is telling the truth. The fifth time the wife swears her oath, the punishment is taken from her.

It also includes those signs which indicate to whom marriage is unlawful because of blood relationship, having been nursed by the same woman, and relationship through marriage.

That which repels whatever corrupts the health of the body and the ability to have children are things which aid the human being in maintaining a healthy body and the ability to reproduce. Things which oppose these are wars with those who are ungrateful to God for their blessings and incitement to war.

They also include inflicting penalties, fines, establishing enhancements, expiations, blood-money and retaliation. Retaliation and blood-money are deterrents against someone destroying or injuring the life of another.

The punishment for theft and robbery are given to repel those who might steal or waylay people preventing thieves from stealing their livelihood and their means of survival and earning a living.

The punishments mentioned for adultery, homosexuality and false accusation are given as these acts prevent the reproduction and continuation of society.

In order to repel those who deny the Truth, war with those who are ungrateful is allowed. Those who deny the Truth bring about disorder in society's means of livelihood and worship, both necessary to draw near to God.

As for the unjust, they should be fought against fiercely to repel the confusion and persecution they might cause because of the outbreak of any dissidents who are beyond the control of the guardians who act on behalf of the Messenger of the Lord of the worlds. And you can therefore go back to the signs provided in this connection in addition to the basics that might be realized by those meditating on the benefits of the Shariah's stipulating the punishments of worldly injunctions.

This section also incorporates the lawful and the prohibited and God's punishments. It is through these signs that the most aromatic of musk is found. These are the comprehensive volume containing the Quranic chapters and signs. These six divisions, then, are the basic principles to be found in the teachings of the Quran and its signs. If you were to collect these six divisions into one corpus, you would find that there are ten different types. They are the divine essence, the divine names and qualities, the divine acts, the world to come, the straight path (the purification of the soul), the situation of the gnostics, the situation of God's enemies, His arguments with the ungrateful, and finally the limits of legal ordinances.

Chapter 4: On how all knowledge branches off from these ten topics and how the knowledge of the Quran is divided into the knowledge of the outer shell and the knowledge of the inner jewels and a description of different types of knowledge

It has now become clear how the knowledge of the Quran relates to these ten divisions of Quranic signs and also the grades of this knowledge in respect to closeness and distance from the goal. Know that the realities that have been indicated have secrets like hidden jewels, hidden in shells. The shell is what appears first. Some people who attain to the shell come to know only this. Others break the shells and then carefully study the pearls hidden in the shell. In the same way, the shell that hides the jewels of the Quran, its apparel, is the Arabic language. From this five branches of knowledge develop.

So from the words of the Quran knowledge of the Arabic language results; from the syntax of the words, knowledge of syntax of Arabic grammar; from the various syntaxes of the Quran, knowledge of reciting; from the pronunciation of

Quranic letters, knowledge of the letters of the alphabet.

This is due to the fact that the first aspect of meaning that is united with speech is sound. Then from the sound comes the letters of the alphabet. The letters are put together to make a word. The gathering of the letters makes the Arabic language. The shaping of the letters gives the quality of syntax.

How one of the various syntaxes makes a recitation results in the seven standard recitations. When syntax is applied to a proper Arabic word, it then indicates a meaning. The meaning calls for an exegesis and this is the fifth form of knowledge.

This is the knowledge of the shell and the outer aspects of the Quran. None of this knowledge, however, is of equal rank. Just as a shell has an internal side that faces the pearls and resembles it to a certain extent because it is continually in contact with the pearl, the shell also is similar to other stones because of its distance from the pearl.

This is the same with the shell of the Quran. Its outer face is sound and relates to a person given the knowledge of correcting its transmission and pronunciation. This is a person who has knowledge of its letters. In this way he has knowledge of the outer which is at a distance from the inner part of the shell as well as the pearl itself.

There is a certain group of people who are so ignorant that they think that the Quran is only letters and sound. They base their theory of the Quran on this and say that it is created since letters and sounds are created. These people most fittingly should be stoned to death or their mind should be stoned. It is not sufficient to reprimand them or to be hard against them because they are a disaster. There is nothing of the world of the Quran and the stations of its heavens that appeared to them except its most distant outer aspect.

With this you have become familiar with the degree of knowledge of the reciter of the Quran because he only knows the correct letters of the alphabet.

Along with this knowledge is the knowledge of the language of the Quran. Included in this are, for example, the translation of the Quran and things similar to that like knowledge of the strange words of the Quran. Then close to this is the knowledge of the syntax of language and this is the syntax of grammar. To a certain extent, this knowledge comes after the knowledge of language because syntax comes after that to which it is applied. Close to that knowledge is the knowledge of recitation. This is a knowledge by which the various forms of syntax and types of pronunciation are made known. It is more important to the Quran than philology and grammar, but it is also among the types of knowledge that are not needed. However philology and grammar are types of knowledge that the human being needs. This is why the philologist and the grammarian are of a higher degree than one who just has knowledge of the recitation. In any case, all these types of people are just turning around the shell and outer aspect of the Quran although they are of different levels.

Along with or close to knowledge of recitation is the knowledge of exegesis of the Quran. This is the final aspect compared to the shell or outer aspect of the Quran. It is closest to the pearl. This is why it even resembles the pearl. Some people even consider that this aspect is the pearl itself, that there is nothing more valuable. That is why most people are satisfied with this amount of knowledge. Yet how they are deprived because they think that there is no knowledge above what they themselves know.

In regard to others who have knowledge of the shell, they are considered to be of a high and noble degree as knowledge of exegesis is high when compared to other knowledge of the shell.

When people attain these five degrees of knowledge, guarding them and transmitting them, God will certainly reward their efforts and purify them. As the Messenger said: May God brighten the face of one who heard my words, then understood them, and performed as they are. It may be that a bearer of knowledge may learn from one who is more knowledgeable or to one who knows less than he. And all those bearers who have heard and performed . . . . (Ibn Majah)

People of these five degrees heard and transmitted and certainly will attain the reward of bearing what they heard and transmitting what they heard to one who is more learned than them or to one who is not learned. The commentator on the Quran who is limited in his exegesis to relating that which is related to him is a bearer and transmitter. In the same way, one who has memorized the Quran and Traditions is a bearer and a transmitter.

Knowledge of the Traditions separates into these aspects of the Quran in addition to its recitation and the pronunciation of the letters. The rank of one who memorizes the Traditions and then teaches them to others is like one who memorizes the Quran and teaches it. The degree of one who knows the external meaning of the Traditions is similar to that of one who has knowledge of exegesis. The degree of one who concentrates on knowledge of the names of the transmitters of Traditions is like the degree of a grammarian or philologist. This is because Traditions are related to us through a chain of transmitters and the narration of the Traditions. Therefore knowledge of the transmitters is like the knowledge of a vehicle and the conditions of a vehicle.

All these types of knowledge can be compared to the shell of the Quran.

The second type is knowledge of the kernel of the Quran.

There are two degrees. The lowest degree is the knowledge of three Quranic categories namely as follows.

The first is the knowledge of the narrations of the Quran and what concerns the Prophets and those who deny God and His enemies. This kind of knowledge is held by story tellers, preachers and some of the transmitters of Traditions. This type of knowledge is not a universal need.

The second is the knowledge of God's Word with those who are ungrateful and His disputation with them. Knowledge of theology comes in this category. This knowledge is to discredit errors and heresies against Islam and to eliminate doubts. This knowledge is held by theologians. This knowledge can be understood through two levels. We have explained the lower level in *The Epistle from Jerusalem* (*al-Risāla al-qudsiyya*) and the higher level in *The Mean in Belief* (*al-Iqtiṣād fī-l iᶜtiqād*).

This knowledge is to guard one's religious belief from what the heretics say. However this kind of knowledge does not center on intuitive knowledge of realities. This kind of knowledge was used in *Incoherence of the Philosophers* (*Tahāfut al-falāsifa*); in *Mustaẓhirī* and *The Proof of the Truth and Fragments of Bāṭinism* (*Ḥujja al-Ḥaqq wa qawāṣim al-bāṭiniyya*) and *The Explanation of Disagreement on the Principles of Religion* (*Mufaṣṣal al-khilāf fī uṣūl al-dīn*). This knowledge makes use of logic by which one learns the means of debate. That is, the method of disputing by true argument. We discussed them in *The Touchstone of Reflection* (*Miḥaqq al-naẓar*) and in *The Standard of Knowledge* (*Miᶜyār al-ᶜilm*). The discussion is such as not to be found in works of jurists or theologians. Whoever is not familiar with these two books will not be aware of what doubt or arguments there are.

The third is knowledge of the legal ordinances that deal

with wealth and women. These relate to one's life and reproduction of life. This knowledge is the knowledge that jurists attain, knowledge known as the issues of mutual relations. Another aspect relates to issues of marriage and reproduction, that is, women. The aspect on crime deals with the restraint necessary for those who cause corruption to either life or reproduction.

There is a universal need for this knowledge because it refers to the blessings of this world and the blessings in the world to come. Those who have this knowledge are known as preachers, story tellers and theologians.

A great deal of research has been done in this area of knowledge, more than is even necessary. Many books have been written on the subject particularly in regard to disputed problems even though disagreeing is allowed in seeking the truth. Whoever strenuously endeavors to reason an issue may be close to being right and earn one reward if he should make a mistake. His opponent is said to have attained two rewards because he is correct. This kind of knowledge led to fame and influence. As a result, many were motivated to develop many branches of this knowledge.

We wasted much of our life writing books on creeds and sorting them out in *The Simple* (*al-Basīṭ*); *The Mediator* (*al-Wasīṭ*) and *The Concise* (*al-Wajīz*). All this served to develop many branches of this kind of knowledge. What we put forward in the book *The Essence of the Abridged* (*Khulāṣa al-mukhtaṣar*) suffices.

That is the fourth book of ours on this branch of knowledge and the smallest of all these works. Legal judgments were given on problems by the early generations but they did not cover any more than what this book contains. Correct judgments were given by them through the grace of God or they suspended judgment saying that they did not know. They did not devote their time to this knowledge. They were devoted to other forms of knowledge. As they were occupied with other things, others came to this knowledge. This is how the knowledge of jurisprudence branched off from the Quran.

The principles of jurisprudence (*uṣūl al-fiqh*) developed from the science of jurisprudence, the Quran and the Traditions. It was a knowledge devoted to the laws of seeking decisions based on the divine law, on Quranic signs and the Traditions.

You should know that the degree or rank of the story teller and preacher was below that of the jurists and theologians. This is because the story tellers and preacher are most often concerned with tales of oral traditions and similar kinds of knowledge. Jurists and theologians are close to each other in degree. However there is a universal need for jurists and even a more universal need for theologians. Both fields are needed in this world. Jurists preserve judgments about food and women and this is necessary. Theologians turn away disputes and arguments of heretics so that their corrupt ways not find sympathetic ears.

In regard to the relationship between jurists and theologians on the journey to God is as this: The jurists can be compared to those who build and provide places of refuge and facilities along the way of the pilgrimage to Mecca . Theologians, on the other hand, can be compared to things spent on the journey of the pilgrimage and they guard the pilgrims. If jurists and theologians had included journeying to God among their occupations by turning away from worldliness, then their degree in comparison to others would be as the sun over the moon. However, if they limit themselves to their occupation, their degree is much lower.

The higher degrees of knowledge of the kernel of the Quran is contained in that knowledge which precedes and is the root of the three types of knowledge mentioned above.

The highest and most noble of this knowledge is knowledge of God and the Last Day for this is the knowledge of what is to come.

This is followed by knowledge of the straight path and the way of journeying upon it. This includes knowledge of how to purify the soul, how to rid oneself of destructive qualities or vices and how to attain constructive qualities or virtues.

This form of knowledge was written about in the forty books of *The Revival of the Religious Sciences*. There the destructive qualities or vices are described in a quarter of the book. These are the qualities that the soul must purify. They include greed, anger, pride, ostentation, conceit, envy, love of influence, love of wealth and so forth. In the quarter on Constructive Qualities the praiseworthy qualities are described which the soul must attain including asceticism, trust in God, satisfaction with divine decrees, love of God, truthfulness, sincerity and so on.

The Revival of the Religious Sciences consists of forty books, each of which will guide a person to one of the obstacles presented by the animal soul along with the treatment in order to remove it. It also describes one of the veils of the animal soul along with how to lift it. This is a knowledge that is above the knowledge of jurisprudence and theology because this is the knowledge of how to journey on the path to God itself while the others are knowledge of the means or vehicles to fix or repair its stations and of repelling those which prevent the journey from taking place.

Among all the types of knowledge, the highest is the knowledge of God. This is the purpose of all the other types of knowledge. This is what is sought by the seeker. The way to progress to it is to begin with the divine acts and from them to the divine names and qualities and finally from there to the divine essence.

There are, then, three stages. The highest and most noble is the knowledge of the divine essence. Most people will not understand this. That is why the command has gone out to them: Reflect on God's creation and do not reflect on His Essence. The Messenger indicated this method when he said: I seek the protection of Thy forgiveness from Thy punishment. (*Sunan al-Nisai*).

This is how he observed the divine acts. Then he said: I seek the protection of Thy pleasure from Thy displeasure. This is his modeling the divine names and qualities. Finally he said: I seek the protection of Thee against Thee. This is his observing the divine essence.

Therefore he was moving step by step toward nearness to God. Just as he moved to reach the extreme station he said of his inability: I do not understand Thy praise; Thou art as Thou hast praised Thyself. (*Sahih Muslim*)

The knowledge of God is the most noble of all types of knowledge. This knowledge is followed by knowledge of the world to come. This is the knowledge of the final return to God as mentioned in the description of the three main categories of the Quran. This knowledge relates to knowledge of gnosis. It refers to knowledge of the human being's relation to God. This includes both knowledge of the relationship to God when being drawn near to Him through knowledge or being veiled from Him through ignorance.

Some of the main points of these four types of knowledge, i.e., knowledge of the divine essence, knowledge of the divine names and qualities, knowledge of the divine acts and knowledge of the world to come and their relationship to each other is that extent of knowledge we have been given in spite of our short life, in spite of many trials and tribulations we face. And we find few people who are helpers or companions.

We did not, however, discuss this in some of our works.

The reason for not mentioning it is that according to most people's understanding, it would only serve to tire them and as for the weak, who are the most traditional in knowledge, they would be harmed by it. It is only beneficial to disclose it to one who has followed the journey to God by removing destructive qualities from his animal soul by undergoing asceticism so that his animal soul becomes trained and is in a good state on the straight path. He is a person who no longer takes any pleasure in the destructive qualities of this world and only searches for the One. Also he is given illuminating insight, critical thinking, a sharp intellect and clear understanding. It is not permissible for this book to be disclosed to any but those who combine all of the above qualities.

This, then are the areas of knowledge that originate in the Quran and their degrees.

Chapter 5: On how previous and present types of knowledge branch off from the Quran

Perhaps you will wonder they I have limited knowledge to only these when there are many other types of knowledge as well like knowledge of the stars, of the forms of the universe, the forms of the body of animals and anatomy of its limbs, knowledge of magic and of talisman, and so on.

Know that we have only mentioned religious knowledge, the existence of the beginning of the universe as this is required so that one may journey on the way to God and so that that journey towards Him may be easy. As to the other types of knowledge which you have mentioned, there is no doubt that they are also types of knowledge but the happiness of this present life and that of the life to come does not rely on knowledge of them. This is the reason why we have not mentioned them. In addition to the types of knowledge you have mentioned there are others as well, the meaning of which are known yet the universe is not empty of those who know them. Therefore there is no need to mention them here.

I would say that with clear insight, insight free from any doubt, it is clear to us that there are many types of knowledge that have not yet come into existence but the possibility and potentiality for them exists. It is in the human being's ability to get hold of them. There are other types of knowledge which came into being but have now been nullified so that at this time not a single person who knows them will be found.

Again, there are still other types of knowledge which some of the angels who are drawn near to God possess but this type of knowledge is beyond the ability of human beings to possess. The human being is limited to a relatively high perfection in this type of knowledge but this is not so with the angels. The type of knowledge that animals can attain is even more limited to the extent of the highest imperfection. It is only God Whose knowledge is not limited in any way.

The knowledge of the human being is limited in comparison to the knowledge of the One in two ways. First of all, there is the negation of its highest rank and secondly, in His case, knowledge is not such as to be in a state of potentiality and possibility just waiting to come into being. Rather, that knowledge already exists and is present. When it comes to the knowledge of God, every possibility of perfection exists.

The aims of those types of knowledge which we have mentioned and of those which we have not mentioned are however not outside the Quran. All of these types of knowledge are pulled out from one of the seas of knowledge of God, that is, the sea of knowledge of His Actions and Deeds.

It has been indicated that the Quran is like a sea that has no shore. As the Quran itself says: *"Say: If the sea had been ink for the Words of my Lord, the sea would come to an end before the Words of my Lord come to an end even if We brought about replenishment the like of it."* (18:109).

Among the acts of God that is referred to because of their vastness are the sea of His acts for health and disease. In narrating the words of Abraham, He said: *"And when I am sick, it is He Who heals me."* (26:80)

This type of knowledge can only be known by one who has knowledge of medicine completely. This knowledge is nothing but the knowledge of all aspects of diseases along with their symptoms and the knowledge of their cure and how to attain to it.

Among the acts of God are the determination of the human being's knowledge of the sun and the moon and of their movement according to a fixed reckoning as God has said: *"The sun and the moon are to keep count."* (55:5). He also said: *"It is He Who made the sun an illumination and the moon as a light and ordained its mansions so that you would know the number of the years and the reckoning."* (10:5). Again, He said: *"But when their sight will be astonished and the moon will cause the earth to e swallowed and the sun and the moon are gathered, the human being will say on that Day: Where is a place to run away to?"* (75:7-10). And: *"He causes the nighttime to be interposed in the daytime and He causes the daytime to be interposed into the nighttime and He causes the moon to become subservient and the moon"*(35:13); and *"Glory be to Him Who created pairs, all of them, of what the earth causes to develop as well as themselves and of what they know not!"* (36:38).

The real meaning in regard to the movement of the sun and the moon according to a fixed reckoning and of the eclipse of both, of how the night and the day merge into one another and how they wrap themselves around one another can only be known by the type of knowledge known as astronomy.

In addition, the meaning of *"O human being! What has deluded you as to your generous Lord, He Who created you, then shaped you in proportion?"*(82:6-8) can only be known by the type of knowledge known as anatomy which includes knowledge of the human being's limbs and internal organs, their number, their kinds, their underlying wisdom and their uses.

God has mentioned these in many signs of the Quran and knowledge of these relates to the knowledge of the past and present day scholars. As a matter of fact, the coming together of these types of knowledge of the past and present day scholars come from the Quran. Just as God has said: I perfected the form of Adam and breathed My Spirit into him. The complete meaning of this cannot be known until the perfection of form, breath and Spirit are known. There are many such obscure types of knowledge related to these, the occupation of which most people do not know of. It can even be that they do not understand these types of knowledge even if they hear them from one who knows them.

If I were to continue to mention the details of divine acts which are indicated in the Quran, it would take a great deal of time. Only a mention of their coming together is appropriate here as we have previously said in this work. That is, that the knowledge of divine acts is part of the total knowledge of God. That total includes these details as well.

Also every category we have mentioned briefly here will branch off into many more details. Think on the Quran then and seek out all of its meanings. In this way perhaps you will come to know the coming together of the types of knowledge of the previous and present peoples and the total of their beginnings.

The reason why one should reflect on the Quran is so

that one may reach from the brief description given here in regard to types of knowledge to a detailed knowledge of the signs which are like an ocean that has no shore.

Chapter 6: On the meaning of the statement that the Quran contains red sulfur, the greatest antidote, the most aromatic musk and all other kinds of precious gems including rubies and pearls. This is only perceived by those who know the relationship between the manifest and the hidden worlds.

It may be that you would say: You have mentioned in some of the categories of types of knowledge that you have given that there are some of the greatest of antidotes to be found in some, the most aromatic musk in others and still in others, red sulfur, as well as other valuables. These are but traditional symbols that give intimations of hidden meanings behind them. Take off the veils of these meanings in order to help me to better understand.

Know that being affected and only following what others have said is hateful to people who are engaged in serious endeavor. In every sentence of the Quran there are intimations of a hidden meaning. This meaning is only understood by one who understands the relationship between the world of perception and the world of the unseen.

This is because everything in the world of perception has something similar in the world of the unseen. This is in regard to its spirit and meaning and not in regard to its form. While the physical form from the world of perception is part of its spiritual meaning of that unseen world, this is the reason why this present world holds one of the stations of the path to God. This station is necessary for the human being. Just as it is not possible to attain the core except through the rind, in the same way it is not possible to move towards the world of spirits except through the outer form of the world of bodies. This relationship can best be known through an example. Reflect on what is shown to a sleeping person in a true dream which is a forty-sixth part of prophethood (*Sahih al-Bukhari*).

This is given to him through imaginative forms. A person who teaches wisdom to ones who are not worthy of it sees in his sleep that he is putting pearls around the necks of pigs. Another person dreams that there is a ring in his hand with which he is sealing women's genitals and the mouths of men.

Ibn Sirin asked in his *The Interpretation of that Dreams*: Are you a person who calls out to formal prayer in the lunar month of Ramadan before dawn. The person answered: Yes. That is so.

Another person dreamed he was pouring oil into olive oil. Ibn Sirin said in his interpretation of that dream: If you have a slave woman, she is in fact your mother. She had been captured in a war and sold. You bought her without knowing your relationship to her. This was the case.

Notice that sealing mouths and genitals with a ring is in concordance with calling out to formal prayer before dawn. This is so because the spirit of the ring is to prohibit even though the former differs from the latter in respect to form. Then compare the other two dreams we have indicated.

Know that within the Quran and the Traditions there are many examples of this type. Reflect on the words of the Prophet: The mind of a believer in God lies between the two fingers of the Merciful. (*Sahih Muslim*). While the spirit of the finger is its ability to engage in rapid movement, the believer's mind is clearly a place of meeting of the angel and of Satan. Satan misleads the person and the angel guides him to the right path. Through these two, that is, the angel and

Satan, God changes the human being's mind just as the human being changes things with his two fingers.

Reflect on how the relationship of these two appointed beings with God, that is, the angel and Satan, correlate to that of your two fingers with the meaning of His two fingers. Yet they differ in form.

Now from this, take out the spiritual meaning of the words of the Prophet: Surely God created Adam in His form (*Sahih al-Bukhari*) and all signs and all other Traditions that the ignorant imagine to show resemblance between the human being and God. It is sufficient for an intelligent human being to be shown one example. Many examples only serve to add to the confusion of fools.

When you understand the meaning of the divine finger, you can move toward the understanding of the divine pen, hand, right hand, face and form. Once you have taken all of these into consideration in their spiritual meaning, not physical meaning, you will come to know what the spirit of the pen and its reality are which one needs to investigate once one has mentioned the definition of pen. This lies in that which is written. Therefore if there is anything in existence through which means the forms of knowledge are engraved on the plates of human souls, it is most suitable that such a thing be called the pen. "*He Who taught by the pen. He taught the human being what he knows not.*" (96:4-5).

The pen being referred to is the spiritual pen because the spirit of the pen and its reality of being a pen are found in it. It is only the form of the pen that does not show it. The reality of being a pen is not because it is made out of wood or a reed. This is the reason why it is not part of the real definition of a pen. Everything that exists has a definition, a reality and that reality is its spirit. When you have discovered the spirit, you have become spiritual. The doors of the unseen world are now open to you and you are now worthy of associating with the Highest Counsel of angels who are the best of companions.

It is possible that these kinds of similitudes are to be found in the Quran even though perhaps you are not able to accept this kind of thing which you hear until you can find an explanation from one of the companions of the Prophet. If blind imitation has its hold over you, consider the commentator's reasoning of the Word of God: "*He sent forth water from heaven and it flowed into valleys according to their measure. Then the flood bears away the front. And from what they kindle in a fire, looking for glitter or sustenance, there is a froth the like of it. Thus God compares the Truth and falsehood. Then as for the froth, it goes as swelling scum while what profits humanity abides on the earth. Thus God propounds parables*" (13:17).

Notice how God has compared knowledge with water, souls with valleys and springs and error with froth. Then at the end of the sign He has made clear to you saying: "*Thus God propounds parables.*" (24:35, 13:17) This is sufficient a depth of discussion on this topic as you are not able to understand more than this.

Know that everything that it is possible that you understand is given to you in the Quran in a way that if in your sleep you were studying the Guarded Tablet with your soul, it would be given to you through a symbol which you would then need to interpret.

It is clear that exegesis of the Quran is similar to the exegesis of dreams. This is the reason why we have indicated that a commentator on the Quran is related to the outer part because to the person who comments and who translates the outer meaning of the ring only, genitals and mouths are not like the person who comprehends that the real meaning is calling out the formal prayer at dawn.

Chapter 7: On the reasons why the entities of the hidden world are explained in the Quran using examples from the manifest world

Why is it that you have explained these realities through hints and symbols but you have not clearly expressed them. It may be that people will assume that you are ignorant of the resemblance and under the influence of the imagination? Know that you will realize this when you come to know that the unseen is made manifest only through symbols from the Guarded Tablet to a person who is sleeping. It is not made manifest through a clear example. I have shown you this in the example I gave.

This is a thing which only becomes known to a person who has understood the connection between the hidden and the manifest worlds. Once you come to know this, you will know that in the present life you are in reality asleep even though you think that you are awake. As the Prophet said: Human beings are asleep. Only when they die will they awaken.

When one awakens at the time of death, what had been meanings and the spirit of the things that they heard in this present life through symbols will become apparent to them. They will then know that those symbols are but outer aspects and shells of these spirits. At that time they will also know with the certainty of conviction in regard to the Quranic signs and the Traditions of the Messenger.

It is similar for the person who called out the formal prayer and who became assured of the truth of Ibn Sirin's words and the truth of his interpretation of the dream. These are the things that become manifest at the time of death.

Sometimes they are made manifest when one is in the throes of death. Those who have been in denial of God and have not obeyed His Messenger will grieve saying: "*On a*

Day when will be turned upside down their faces in the fire, they will say: O would that we had obeyed God and obeyed the Messenger!" (33:66). God also said in this regard: *"Are they looking for nothing but its interpretation? The Day its interpretation approaches, those who had forgotten it before will say: Surely Messengers of our Lord drew near us with the Truth. Have we any intercessors who will intercede for us? Or will we be returned so that we would do other than what we were doing before? Surely they have lost themselves. Gone astray from them is what they had been devising."* (7:53). And *"Ah! Woe is me! Would that I had not taken so-and-so to myself as a friend! Certainly he has caused me to go astray from the Remembrance after it had drawn near to me. And Satan had been a betrayer of the human being."* (25:28) or *"We have warned you of a near punishment on a Day when a man will look on what his hands have put forward and the ones who are ungrateful will say: O would that I had been earth dust!"* (78:40) and *"so that a soul may not say: Woe to me that I am regretful for what I neglected in my responsibility to God and that I had truly been among the ones who deride."* (39:56) or *"Surely those have lost who have denied the meeting with God until when the Hour draws near to them suddenly, they would say: What a regret for us that we neglected in it!"* (6:31) and *"And if you but see when the ones who sin become ones who bend down their heads before their Lord: Our Lord! We have perceived and heard. So return us as ones who will act in accord with morality. Truly we are now ones who are certain."* (32:12). Most of these Signs relate to the description of the life to come or the world to come. We call these signs green olivine.

Know then that as long as you are in this present life, you are asleep. You will only awaken at the time of death. At that time it will be possible for you to see The Truth with clarity. Until that time, the realities of that world can only be known through the form of symbols expressed through the faculty of imagination. As you tend to concentrate on what the senses reveal to you, you believe that the senses only present meaning through imagination. You fail to recognize its spirit. You neglect your own spirit and only recognize your body.

Chapter 8: On comprehending the relationship between the manifest and hidden worlds

It may be that you say: Tell us the relationship between the two worlds. Tell us why a dream speaks to us through symbols and not through clear examples. Why was it that the Messenger of God was to see Gabriel in a form other than the form of Gabriel and he only saw him two times in his own form?

Know that if you assume that you will be given this knowledge without any preparation for it, you are being proud and arrogant. Preparation includes discipline in morality, mortification, renunciation of the destructive qualities of this world completely, running away from preoccupation with human beings, becoming devoted in the love of the Creator and seeking the One. This knowledge will not be given to person like yourself.

Leave aside your desire to obtain this knowledge by vicarious correspondence. It can only be sought through the door of mortification and Godfearingness. At that time guidance will appear and give it strength. God has said: "*And as for those who struggled for Us, We will truly guide them to Our ways. And truly God is with the ones who are doers of good.*" (29:69) The Prophet said: Whoever acts upon what he knows, God will grant him the knowledge of what he does not know.

Know for sure that the secrets of the manifest world are veiled from souls that are filled with love for this present life and who devotes most of his energies in pursuing the present world. We have only indicated so much of the secrets so that we would create a yearning for them. We hoped to encourage one to want to attain to them. It is to show one of the secrets of the Quran to someone is ignorant of them. It is for the person to whom the shells of the Quran have not opened to reveal its jewels. If a person's intention is sincere, that person will try to find those secrets.

Also, it has been mentioned to show one of the secrets of the Quran. Those who are heedless of this secret can not realize the pearls hidden in the Quran (that is, the deep meanings of the Quran). When one has the intention to do so, he should exert much effort and seek the help of those who are well-versed in the religious knowledge. One cannot be successful in this field with the help of his limited reason.

How can one understand these deep meanings with the help of his finite mind? The one who has such idea has never understood the meaning of the Quranic sign in which God the Almighty says, *"There is not a thing but it glorifies His praise, but you understand not their glorification"* (17:44) or the Quranic sign in which God, Exalted be He, says, *"Approach . . . . willing or unwilling,"* (41:11) can never realize the deep meanings and the hidden secrets of the Quran unless you realize that the earth speaks a language and is alive. Once one said: A wall said to a peg: "Why are you digging through me?" The peg replied: "Ask the one that is hammering me and not leaving me. The stone that hammers me is behind me." Such speech is more truthful than people's speech. How then can one understand the secrets behind that?

Chapter 9: On the description of the symbols underlying red sulfur, the greatest antidote, the most aromatic musk, pearls and so on

It may be that you wish to become aware of the symbols

and references that appear under the jewels that are included in the Quran as we have described.

One should know that the red sulfur, as it is called in this worldly life, is the substance through which worthless minerals are turned into valuable ones; stones into rubies and copper into gold so that the human being can enjoy the finite and temporary pleasures of this worldly life.

Is it not better to give the name of red sulfur to that which turns people's hearts from the darkness of ignorance and animality to the purity and spirituality of angels, from the lowest rank to the most superior one? Is the Quran through which one can grow closer to God, the Lord of the worlds, and enjoy the blessings of seeing the Countenance of God forever? Should the name of this be that of red sulfur or not?

This is why it is better to give the Quran the name of red sulfur. Consider with deep reflection. Ask yourself if this makes sense. Be fair. In this way you should come to know that this name is the most worthy of this meaning and the best application of it. The most precious thing to be attained through knowledge of alchemy is the ruby. That is the reason why we named it knowledge of divine essence.

As for the great antidote, it is a cure for all deadly poisons. Death resulting from such poisons is no more than an end to this temporary life.

Now, consider the poisons of heresy, deviation and deception existing in one's heart which prevent the human being from realizing the world of spiritualities forever. However, the Quran is a cure for all such poisons and can discard their harm. Isn't better to give the Quran the name of the great antidote?

Regarding musk, the Quran is like something that accompanies a person to the world to come from which a powerful aroma of musk is sent out. Even if one tries to hide it, it cannot be hidden. Its scent is spread everywhere. Thus, one should take into consideration the worldly branches of knowledge. If one is well-versed in one of the branches of knowledge of this worldly life, such knowledge can raise his name to be a lofty name even if he tries to hide it and prefers laziness. Thus the name of musk is better to be given to him, is not it? You know that when one is strongly established in jurisprudence and Islamic juristic rulings, such practice perfume one's name, make one famous and grants one grandeur. It is a fact that what is realized by one's good reputation and the spread of his grandeur is even better than the good smell of musk.

As for aloeswood, it is of no use as long as it is not burned. However, when aloeswood is thrown into a fire, it sends an aromatic smell. This can apply to the hypocrites and the enemies of God who are like wood. When God punishes them by sending thunderbolts, earthquakes and other catastrophes, they are burnt and smoke rises from them and reaches the noses of heedless people. As a result, they become more interested in seeking God's pleasure and the Garden. In addition, they keep themselves away from deviation and heedlessness. This is what is referred to as aloeswood.

I am satisfied with explaining these symbols, giving you the chance to deduce the meaning of remaining symbols and to be one of those who can do so easily. Surely, those to whom I call will hear if he is still alive. But alas, he seems to be as one who has gone and lost his life.

Chapter 10: On the benefits of these signs

One may say: It seems to me that these symbols are true. Are there any other benefits of such symbols?

One should know that such symbols are replete with benefits. This is a way to know the spiritual and deep meanings of words in order to be able to fathom the depths of the Quran so that you can attain the hidden meanings of the signs of the Quran. Some people may be confused by some phenomena and controversial matters. This has led them to disbelieve in the Day of Judgment, the Garden, hellfire and the resurrection.

As a result, they took off the garment of piousness and Godfearingness. Moreover, they have indulged in satisfying their lusts and seeking the forbidden worldly pleasures. Also, they became more interested in seeking money, grandeur and temporary pleasures. They also underestimated those who are pious and looked at them contemptuously. Whenever they realize the piety of those whom they cannot deny for their affluent knowledge, perfect reason and deep thinking, they claim that those pious people seek to confuse people and attract them. As a result, realizing the piousness of those people leads them to be more deviant and more misleading although realizing the piousness of people is one of the things that confirm the beliefs of the believers.

This is because those misleading people consider the external appearance and imaginary mold of things. They never fathom the depths and realities of things. In addition, they have not realized the balance between this worldly life and the world to come. As a result, they have gone astray.

Rather, they have misled others. They have neither realized the spiritual world as have the pious people nor believed in the unseen world like ordinary people.

Consequently their intelligence has led them to destruction. It is a fact that ignorance is better to salvation than destructive intelligence. This is a fact as we ourselves went astray for a period of time because of bad companions, but God the Almighty has willed to keep us away from their slips and faults.

All thanks to God the Almighty Who has guided us to the right path as this cannot be realized by mere efforts and wishing. God the Almighty says: *"Whatever God may open of mercy to humanity, there is not one who holds it back and what He holds back, there is not one who sends it after that."* (35:2)

Chapter 11: On the excellence of some signs of the Quran more than others when they are all the Word of God

One may say: Some signs of the Quran are preferred over others although they are all the Word of God. How are some signs preferred over others?

One should know that if the light of insight does not guide you to the difference between some signs of the Quran and between some chapters of the Quran and you fear your soul that incites to evil, you should imitate the Prophet to whom the Quran was revealed. There are prophetic traditions showing that some signs are preferred over others and given more reward than others. God's Messenger said: The Opening Chapter is the best of the chapters of the Quran. He also said: The "Throne" sign (2:255) is the master sign of the Quran. The Prophet said: Chapter 36 (Ya Sin) is the heart of the Quran and Chapter 112 (The Sincere Expression) equals one-third of the Quran. Moreover, narrations regarding the recitation of these signs and chapters are countless. You can find the prophetic Traditions in the books of *Ahadith*.

Now we turn to the meaning of these four Traditions that speak of the excellence of these signs or chapters. The way the Quran is arranged and the divisions of it, its branches and its grades will also help you understand this meaning. Review them and think about them. As we have mentioned, we have branched out the categories of the Quran into ten topics.

Chapter 12: On the mysteries of the Opening Chapter and how it contains eight of the ten kinds of precious gems of the Quran and the description of part of the meaning of The Merciful, the Compassionate in relationship to the nature of animals

Reflecting on the Opening Chapter, one should notice that although is short and concise, it includes eight paths. First, when God the Almighty says: *"In the Name of God, The Merciful, The Compassionate"* (1:1), this is a manifestation of His divine Essence. Second, when God, Glorious be He, says: *"The Merciful, The Compassionate,"* it is a manifestation of one of God's names and qualities. Such name and quality entails the other names and qualities of God the Almighty. Rather, such names and qualities are relevant to the creatures as it shows that God is merciful to them, a matter that urges them to obey God and seek God's Pleasure. This does not apply to the name and quality of anger. Unlike the attribute of mercy, the attribute of anger causes people to be frightened, sad and depressed.

When God, Exalted be He, says: *"The Praise belongs to God, Lord of the worlds,"* (1:2) this entails two things. First: The basis of praise is gratitude. Being grateful is the first step to the right path.

Practical faith is composed of two things: Patience and gratitude. You can refer to the book, *Revival of the Religious Sciences* in the section on "Patience and Gratitude" to know the reality of this point. The preference of gratitude over patience is like the preference of mercy over anger. This is because gratitude results from being content, longing and love of God, whereas patience results from fear, fright, distress and calamities.

Proceeding through the right path of God through love of God is better than proceeding through it through fright and fear of God. One can know this by reading the section "On Love, Longing and Contentment" in the book *Revival of the Religious Sciences*. Thus, the Prophet said: Those who praise God the Almighty in all situations are the first to be called to Paradise.

Second: When God the Almighty says: *"Lord of the worlds,"* this is a reference to all actions and deeds. The words, *"Lord of the worlds"* are the best to show the fact that God is the disposer of all actions and deeds. There is no doubt that the words *"Lord of the worlds"* is better than the word "the Supreme of the worlds" or the "the Creator of the worlds." This is because the term "lordship" is better to refer to the greatness of God, Exalted be He, than other terms.

When God says again: *"The Merciful, The Compassionate,"* (1:3) this is a manifestation of the quality of mercy for the second time. One should not think that this is a sort of repetition. There are no repetitions in the Quran unless such repetition entails extra benefits. The repetition of the quality of mercy after the phrase *"Lord of the worlds"* entails two great benefits.

First: The first merit is relevant to the creatures. God the Almighty has created all in a perfect way and given them what they need. The world of animals is one of the worlds created by God. Also, the worlds of mosquitoes, flies, spiders and bees are the smallest of the worlds created by God, Glorious be He.

Look at the mosquito and how God the Almighty has created its organs. God, Exalted be He, has created in the mosquito with all the organs found in an elephant. In addition, a mosquito has a trunk like that of the elephant with a sharp head through which it can get its food from the blood of human kind. A mosquito pierces its trunk into a person's body and sucks its blood. It has two wings to fly when a person wants to hit it.

Also, consider the world of flies and how God the Almighty has created the organs of a fly. God has created the fly without eyelids as its small head cannot bear eyelids. It is a scientific fact that eyelids protect eyes from dirt and dust. However, God the Almighty has given it two extra arms with which a fly can clean its pupils. Thus, a fly has four legs and two arms.

Regarding the world of spiders, God the Almighty has created a spider with wonderful limbs and taught it how to weave and to catch flies and insects although it cannot fly. God has given it sticky saliva through which it can stick itself to a wall and watch the flies flying near it. Whenever a fly gets near, the spider throws itself on a fly and ties it with its web. As a result, a fly cannot escape. One should consider how a spider weaves its web in a hexagonal shape.

Also, one should consider the world of bees and their wonders regarding the process of collecting honeycomb and wax. Also, one should regard how bees build their houses. A bee builds its house in a hexagonal shape not to narrow the space available for its companions. In case such houses were built as circles, there would be useless spaces between such houses. All geometrical figures produce useless spaces when they are put beside one another with the exception of a hexagon and a square.

Also, the body of the bee is circular so there would be useless spaces inside its house if it were built as a square. Thus, its house takes the shape of a hexagon. This is known as the geometrical proof. Consider how God the Almighty has guided bees to adopt such shape on building their houses. This is undoubtedly an example of God's wonders in this world. It shows how God, Exalted be He, is Merciful with all His creatures. Such wonders cannot be discovered for long periods of time. The lowest in rank is a proof of the most supreme of all creatures.

This means that the wonders found out by humans are very few when compared with the wonders that have not yet been discovered and those known only by God and His angels. One can obtain more information about topics likes these in the chapter "On Patience and Gratitude" and the chapter "On Love, Longing and Contentment" (in the *Revival of the Religious Sciences*). One should seek such useful knowledge. Otherwise one may overlook God's Mercy and preoccupy oneself with useless branches of knowledge such as the poems by al-Mutannabi, the odd grammatical rules by Sibawayh, the funny divorce stories by Ibn al-Haddad or other useless branches of knowledge.

Surely, one's worth is estimated in accordance with one's exerted efforts. God, Exalted be He, says: *"And my advice will not profit you even if I wanted to advise you if God had been wanting to lead you into error."* (11:34) He the Almighty also says: *"Whatever God may open of mercy to humanity, there is not one who holds it back and what He holds back, there is not one who sends it after that."* (35:2) The purpose of this discussion is to give an example of God's Mercy with His creatures.

Second: This sign is related to the following sign in which God the Almighty says: *"One Who is Sovereign of the Day of Judgment"* (1:4) It refers to God's mercy with His creatures on the Day of Judgment when He confers His blessings on those who worship and obey Him.

Thus, the purpose of this discussion is to show that there are no repetitions in the Quran. In case one thinks that a sign is apparently repeated, one should look at the preceding and the following signs to get the idea.

As for the Quranic sign in which God the Almighty says: *"One Who is Sovereign of the Day of Judgment"* (1:4), it is a reference to the Day of Judgment. Belief in the Day of Judgment is one of the fundamentals of the Islamic faith. It refers to some of the qualities of majesty of God the Almighty such as sovereignty and kingdom.

Regarding the Quranic sign in which God the Almighty says: *"And Thee alone we worship and to Thee alone we pray for help"* (1:5) these words include two great pillars. First: It refers to sincere worship which is the spirit of the right path, as shown in the chapter "On Truthfulness and Sincerity" and the chapter on "On the Treatment of Hypocrisy" in the *Revival of the Religious Sciences*.

Second: One should believe that none is worthy to be worshiped except God. This is the core of the belief of monotheism. Such monotheism can be realized through the human being's belief that God is the disposer of all affairs and that one cannot do anything without seeking God's Help. The sign saying: *"Thee alone we worship"* is a reference to beautifying one's soul with worship and sincerity. As for the part of the sign saying: *"to Thee alone we pray for help"* is a reference to purifying one's soul of all forms of disbelief.

As mentioned above, the process of proceeding through the right path is divided into two sections: First: Purifying through negating what should not be done. Second: Beautifying through realizing what should be done, a matter that is included in two words of the Opening Chapter.

Regarding the Quranic sign in which God the Almighty says: *"Guide us to the straight path,"* (1:6) it is a request and a supplication. This is the core of worship, as shown in the section "On Remembrance of Death" in the *Revival of Religious Sciences* where there is a reference to the human need of supplicating to God the Almighty all the time, as supplication is the core of worship. There is a reference to the human need for guidance to the right path of Islam through which one can grow nearer to God, Glorious be He.

As for the Quranic sign in which God the Almighty says: *"The path of those to whom Thou hast been gracious, not the ones against whom Thou art angry nor the ones who go astray"* (1:6-7) it is to remind people of God's blessings on obedient servants and His displeasure and anger with disobedient ones in order to urge people to obey him and warn them against disobeying Him. It has been mentioned that the narration of the stories of prophets and enemies of God represents two great sections of the Quran.

The Opening Chapter includes eight of the ten sections of the Quran:

1. Essence of God
2. Divine names and qualities
3. Divine acts
4. Day of Judgment
5. The straight path with its two meanings: Purifying and beautifying
6. God's satisfaction with obedient servants
7. God's anger with disobedient servants
8. Day of Resurrection

Only two sections are not mentioned in the Opening Chapter. Those two sections are:

A. Arguments against the disbelievers

B. Juristic rulings, the two branches from which scholastic theology and jurisprudence are derived.

However, these two branches are included in the lowest of the ranks of religious sciences. They have been raised to a higher level because of the love of money and the influence they may have.

Chapter 13: On the eight doors to the Garden and how they are opened through the Opening Chapter and that it has the keys to all of them

The Opening Chapter of the Quran is a key to Paradise.

It is a key to Paradise, as the gates of Paradise are eight and the meanings of this Chapter refers to eight things. One should be certain that each sign of the Opening Chapter is a key to Paradise as mentioned in the reported religious narrations. If you do not believe that the Opening Chapter is a key to Paradise but you want to come to know the relationship between them, then you have to leave aside whatever you have understood as the outer aspects of Paradise.

Each section of the Opening Chapter refers to a branch of knowledge, as shown in the section on God's mercy and wonders of creation.

Do not think that the soul of a person who seeks religious knowledge is less pleasant than the soul of the one who seeks to satisfy his lusts and realize the worldly pleasures. How can they be equal? It cannot be denied that the desire of those well-versed in religious knowledge to seek knowledge may be more than their desire to satisfy their basic needs. A religiously knowledgeable person wishes to share the angels in Paradise, as the angels are created to worship God, seeking no worldly pleasures.

Animals may enjoy the worldly pleasures more than human beings. So, if you think that sharing animals in such worldly pleasures it is better to be sought than sharing angels in enjoying the pleasure of seeing God's Countenance in the Hereafter, you are ignorant and straying.

If eight branches of religious knowledge are available for the gnostic and they act upon them paying no attention to the worldly pleasures sought by idiot people, they will enter Paradise which is given as a reward to those endowed with intellect.

As for those who exert much effort only to seek worldly pleasures like animals and do not deny that Paradise is realized by way of seeking all branches of knowledge. If the stations of gnosis do not deserve to be named as paradises, then they can be a key to Paradise. It cannot be denied that the Opening Chapter includes some keys to all gates of Paradise.

Chapter 14: On why the sign of the "Throne" (2:255) is regarded as the major sign of the Quran and why this is so rather than Q3:18, 112:1, 57:1-6, 59:22-24 and all other signs

The Prophet said: The sign of the "Throne" is the master of signs. It may be said: Can one think of why the sign of the "Throne" (2:255) is named the master sign of the Quran? In case one is unable to deduce the reason, one may refer to the sections and ranks mentioned above. It has been mentioned that getting acquainted with God, His essence and His names and qualities is the supreme purpose of the Quranic sciences. All other sections are sought to realize God's essence. God's pleasure is to be sought by all. The sign of the "Throne" is the only Quranic sign which includes the mentioning of God's essence, His names and qualities and His acts.

The part of the sign beginning "*God*" is a reference to the essence of God the Almighty.

The part of the sign saying: "*There is no god but He,*" is a reference to the unity of essence.

The part of the sign saying: "*The Living, The Eternal,*" is a reference to the name and quality of majesty. These names and qualities denote that God, glorious be He, is the Ever-Living, the Superb Upright Sustainer.

As for the part of the sign saying: "*Neither slumber takes Him nor sleep,*" it is a sort of glorifying and sanctifying God the Almighty. It also shows that God is exalted above all qualities of creatures. It is worth mentioning that sanctification is one of the areas of religious knowledge; moreover, it is the most outstanding of these areas.

Regarding the part of the sign saying: *"to Him belongs whatever is in the heavens and whatever is in and on the earth,"* it is evidence that to God belongs all that is in the heavens and in the earth. Rather, it is evidence that to God all creatures will definitely return.

As for the part of the sign saying: *"who would intercede with Him but with His permission?"* it is a reference to the fact that to God belongs sovereignty, disposal of all affairs and the right of intercession. It is also a negation of setting up associates to God the Almighty in His creation and rule.

Concerning the part of the sign saying: *"He knows what is in front of them and what is behind them and they will not comprehend anything of His knowledge but what He willed,"* it is a reference to the quality of knowledge. It also shows that God is unique in His knowledge. Even some have affluent knowledge, such knowledge has been granted to them by God the Almighty.

The part of the sign saying: *"His seat encompassed the heavens and the earth,"* is a reference to the greatness of God's Sovereignty and Ability. There is a secret in this part, which none has realized yet. The knowledge about the seat, its description and how it embraces the heavens and the earth is still a mysterious branch of knowledge for all. It is worth mentioning that many branches of knowledge are related to such branches of knowledge.

As for the part of the sign saying: *"and He is not hampered by their safe keeping,"* is a reference to the quality of ability and perfection of God, as opposed to weakness and imperfection.

Regarding the part of the sign saying: *"And He is The Lofty, The Sublime,"* it is a reference to two great qualities of God. It is worth mentioning that explaining the meaning of those two attributes would require a great deal of time. It has been explained in detail in the book, *The Most Beautiful Names of God* (*al-Maqṣad al-asmā fi asmāʾ Allāh al-ḥusnā*). One can get more information on these two qualities from that book.

If one considers all the meanings included in this Quranic sign and then recites all the signs of the Quran including all meanings of monotheism, sanctification and explanation of God's sublime qualities, one can not find a sign containing all these meanings with the exception of this sign. Thus, the Prophet said: The sign of the "Throne" is the master sign of the Quran.

The sign saying: *"God bears witness that there is no god but He,"* (3:18) includes nothing but Islamic monotheism, whereas the sign saying: *"Say: He is God, the One!"* (112:1) includes nothing but Islamic monotheism and sanctification of God the Almighty. As for the sign saying: *"Say: O God! The One Who is Sovereign of Dominion,"* (3:26) it entails nothing but God's acts and supreme ability.

Regarding the Opening Chapter, it offers symbols of such qualities without explanation, whereas such qualities are explained in detail in the sign of the "Throne." The last signs of Chapter 59 and the first signs of Chapter 57 are similar to the sign of the "Throne," but there are many Signs, not a single sign like this one. Such it is regarded as the master sign of the Quran. Thus, the Prophet said: The sign of the "Throne" is the master of signs in the Quran.

Moreover, it includes the greatest names of God which are the Living, the Eternal. According to some religious narrations, such names are only found in this sign and the first signs of Chapter 3 and the Quranic saying: *"And faces will be humbled before the Living, the Eternal."* (20:111)

Chapter 15: On why the Chapter of Sincere Expression (112) is valued as a third of the Quran

As for the saying of the Prophet: Chapter 112 equals one third of the Quran, I think you cannot understand the reason beyond this tradition. Sometimes you say he mentioned it to arouse the interest for reciting and he did not mean the amount. God forbid that the Prophet intended such a meaning. Sometimes one says this is far from being interpreted or understood and that the Quran consists of more than 6000 signs. How can this little amount equal one third of the Quran? This is because one knows nothing about the essence of the Quran and considers it through words whether long or short, just like the one who prefers many dirhams to one valuable jewel.

One has to know that Chapter 112 definitely equals one third of the Quran. One can resort to the three parts we mentioned about the categories of the Quran, i.e. to obtain a thorough knowledge of God, the world to come and to know the right path. These three categories are fundamental. Anything else is subordinate. Chapter 112 includes one of these three: The knowledge of God and to acknowledge his monotheism and to sanctify Him without associating anyone with Him. This negates anything like unto Him.

To describe God with Self-Sufficiency is to denote that there is none resorted to in need except to Him alone though there is no mention of the world to come nor the straight path therein while we stated that the most important goals of the Quran is to know God, the world to come and the straight path. That is why it equals one third of the Quran, i.e. one third of the fundamentals of the Quran as the Prophet said: The pilgrimage is Arafat. That is, to stay the ninth day of Dhul-Hijjah in Arafat, the Prophet meant that this is the most important rite in the pilgrimage and all other rites are subsidiary.

Chapter 16: On why Chapter Ya Sin (36) is regarded as the heart of the Quran

One seems to be eager to grasp the meaning of the Prophetic Tradition in which the Prophet said: Chapter 36 is the heart of the Quran. I want you to understand it by yourself and use your own inference as you were informed before in such like matters. I hope your can get the meaning. To use your mind and be active in deducing and understanding by yourself is far better than being instructed by anyone else. I hope too that if you get one secret by yourself, you will be more active in using your mind and thought to deduce more and more. By doing so you will know more about the real essence and meanings of the Quran in addition to what we will provide you with to make it easy for you to deduce much more secrets.

Chapter 17: On why the Prophet specified the Opening Chapter as the best chapter of the Quran and the sign of the "Throne" as the major sign of the Quran and the reason why this sign was better than its opposites

One may say: Why is the sign of the "Throne" described to be the master of signs and the Opening Chapter to be the best? Is there any secret or is it agreed upon? Just like when one praises a person, he may use some words and if he praises another person he may use other words?

It can be said that this is far from being right. What you mentioned is uttered by one like me and you who have shortcomings. However if it comes to the Prophet it is something totally different for he speaks in accordance with revelation. Do not think that what is said by him in his various states whether pleasure or anger is but right? The secret beyond this specification is that if something consists of many good qualities, it is called "a better thing," but if something else has many more good merits, it is called "the best." So the best is the one that has more good attributes.

As for the predominance, it means honor and rejects any kind of dependence. If you revise all the meanings we cited about the two, you will know that the Opening Chapter includes many different meanings and connotations so it is considered the best. As to the the sign of the "Throne," it contains the great knowledge of God which is the most important thing in religion and all other branches of knowledge come later. Therefore, it is proper to call it the master.

So be careful of this type of understanding the signs of the Quran in order to attain a deep knowledge and open up your mind. Then you will see more miracles and signs and will enter the paradise of knowledge which has no borders because knowledge of God has now limits.

The paradise you know was created out of borders, even if it they were vast. It has an end for it is impossible to create an infinite body. Never exchange that which is better for that which is lower in order not to be of the common people even if you would be of those admitted to the Garden. The Prophet said: The most inhabitants of the Garden are of the common people, but the most elevated people in it are the people of insight and understanding.

Chapter 18: On the condition of the knowers (gnostics) in this world

One should know that if one's eagerness to meet God and to become acquainted with God's greatness and grandeur is stronger than one's need of food and sex, one will prefer the garden of knowledge to the satisfaction of basic needs.

One should know that this desire has been created in gnostics and not in you because your desire for worldly pleasures is greater in you in the same way the desire for prestige has been created for adults and not for children.

Children have been given the lust for play. One may wonder at the children's love to spend much time playing with one another. Thus they never think of the lust for leadership.

At the same time, a gnostic is surprised at your concern for this world which is all play to the gnostic. When a desire is created in gnostics for this world, their knowledge is in proportion to their desire. This desire of gnostics is not in any way related to sensuous desires. This is because sensuous desires disappear while the other does not. The desire of the gnostics does not sense weariness whereas the latter does.

Unlike other desires for the sensual, desire for the spiritual increases day after day according to the knowledge one attains day after day. However, such desire is similar to the sexual lust that is only created in the human being after maturity. The person who does not have this desire is either like an immature boy whose natural disposition has not been perfected or like that of an impotent person whose natural disposition was corrupted by the difficulties of the world and its desires. When the gnostic receives the desire for gnosis and the pleasure of growing near to God, "*And compete with one another for forgiveness from your Lord and for a Garden whose depth is as the heavens and the earth,"* (3:133) *"its clusters, ones that draw near,"* (69:23) *"and by outspread water and many sweet fruit,"* (69:23). There is no exhaustion in gnosis.

The gnostics look at those who are indulged in their physical lusts in the same way adults look at children who are indulged in their play. Thus they love isolation and seclusion. They avoid prestige and wealth and preoccupy themselves with offering supplication. They turn away from their families and children to invoke God, exalted be he.

Thus, people mock at them all the time, thinking they are insane. However, they themselves mock at people who are indulged in worldly pleasures and physical lusts, saying as mentioned in the Quranic sign: *"He said: If you deride us, then we will deride you just as you deride us."* (11:38) *"And you will know to whom will approach a punishment covering with shame and on whom an abiding punishment will alight!"* (11:39).

Gnostics are preoccupied with preparing a means of rescue for their own selves and for others. This is because they know the dangers of the Day of Judgment. Thus, they mock at those who are heedless in the same way adults mock at children when they are preoccupied with play while a tyrant person is invading their country and wants to kill some and banish others.

One may wonder at the one who is preoccupied with his worthless money and moral sovereignty, paying no attention to the beauty of the divine majesty and grandeur. Nothing prevents hearts from being preoccupied with such beauty after purifying them from all physical lust with the exception of the endless Light of God the Almighty. Glorious be to the One Who has veiled Himself from the eyes of all creatures with His Light.

You poor people are occupied with the influence of this present world while with little wealth you are in awe when these make you content. You forget to look at the beauty and glory of your Lord even though it is illuminating. It becomes apparent to you that because it is so luminous, it need not be sought. It is to present to you that it does not require any reflection. After the soul has been purified from the blameworthy and destructive qualities of this present life, nothing prevents it from occupying itself with the beauty except the weakness of the pupils of the eye. Glory be to Him Who disappears from the sight of people by His very light. He becomes veiled from them by His very Presence.

Chapter 19: On the reason for separating the rubies from the pearls in the Quran

Let's organize the rubies of the Quran on one string and its pearls on another. However, some signs may include both rubies and pearls.

The first half of the Opening Chapter offers some rubies, whereas the other half presents some pearls. As mentioned in a sacred tradition, God the Almighty says: "I have divided the Opening Chapter into two halves between Me and My servant."

It is worth mentioning that the string of rubies refers to the light of knowledge of God (His essence, His names and qualities and His acts), whereas the string of pearls refers to the human being's good acts and deeds. Thus, the first is related to knowledge, whereas the second is related to actions and deeds. Human faith is based on both knowledge and actions.

Part 2: The Rubies of the Quran

The Rubies are those signs concerned with the essence of God, His names and qualities, and His acts. The Rubies of the Quran are 763 signs. This is the cognitive part.

Chapter 1: The Opening 7 Signs

(1:1) In the Name of God, The Merciful, The Compassionate, (1:2) The Praise belongs to God, Lord of the worlds, (1:3) The Merciful, The Compassionate, (1:4) One Who is Sovereign of the Day of Judgment. (1:5) Thee alone we worship and to Thee alone we pray for help. (1:6) Guide us on the straight path, (1:7) the path of those to whom Thou hast been gracious, not ones against whom Thou art angry, nor the ones who go astray.

Chapter 2: The Cow 14 Signs

(2:22) It is He Who assigned the earth for you as a place of restfulness and the heaven as a canopy. And He sent forth water from heaven and drove out fruit of trees by it as a provision for you; then assign not rivals to God while you know.

(2:29) It is He Who created for you all that is in and on the earth. After that He turned His attention to the heaven. Then He shaped them into seven heavens. And He is Knowing of everything.

(2:32) They said: Glory be to Thee! We have no knowledge but what Thou hast taught us; truly Thou, Thou alone art The Knowing, The Wise.

(2:107) Knowest thou not that God, to Him is the dominion of the heavens and the earth, and not for you other than God is there either a protector nor a helper.

(2:115) And to God belongs the East and the West. So wherever you turn to, then after that there is the Countenance of God. Truly God is One Who Embraces, Knowing.(2:116) And they said: God has taken to Himself a son, glory be to Him; nay! To Him belongs whatever is in the heavens and the earth; all are ones who are morally obligated to Him, (2:117) Beginner of the heavens and the earth; and when He decrees a command, then truly He says to it: Be! Then it is!

(2:137) So if they have believed the like of what you have believed in it, then surely they were truly guided; and if they have turned away, then they are not but in breach; so God will suffice for you against them. And He is The Hearing, The Knowing. (2:138) Our coloring is by God; and who is fairer at coloring than God; and we are ones who worship Him.

(2:163) And your God is One God; there is no god but He, The Merciful, The Compassionate. (2:164) Truly in the creation of the heavens and the earth and the alteration of the nighttime and the daytime and the boats that run on the sea, with what profits humanity and what God sent forth from heaven of water and gave life to the earth after its death and disseminated on it all moving creatures and diversified the winds and the clouds that are caused to be subservient between heaven and earth are the signs for a folk who are reasonable.

(2:186) And when My servants ask thee about Me, then truly I am near; I answer the call of one who calls when he calls to Me; so they should respond to Me and believe in Me that perhaps they would be on the right way.

(2:255) God! There is no god but He, The Living, The Eternal. Neither slumber takes Him nor sleep. To Him belongs whatever is in the heavens and whatever is in and on the earth, who is there who would intercede with Him but with His permission? He knows what is in front of them and what is behind them; and they will not comprehend anything of His knowledge, but what He willed. His Seat encompassed the heavens and the earth; and He is not hampered by their safe keeping. And He is The Lofty, The Sublime. (2:256) There is no compulsion in the way of life; surely right judgment has become clear from error. So whoever disbelieves in false deities and believes in God then surely he holds fast to the most firm handhold. It is not breakable, and God is Hearing, Knowing.

Chapter 3: The Family of Imran 13 Signs

(3:1) Alif Lām Mīm. (3:2) God! There is no god but He, The Living, The Eternal. He sent down to thee the Book with The Truth, that which establishes as true what was before it. (3:3) And He has sent forth the Torah and the Gospel before this as a guidance for humanity; (3:4) and He has sent forth the Criterion between right and wrong, truly those who are ungrateful for the signs of God, for them is a severe punishment, and God is Almighty, Possessor of Requital. (3:5) Truly God, nothing is hidden from Him in or on the earth nor in heaven. (3:6) It is He Who forms you in the wombs how He will. There is no god but He, Almighty, Wise.

(3:18) God bears witness that there is no god but He, as do the angels and those who have knowledge, the ones who uphold equity. There is no god but He, The Almighty, The Wise. (3:19) Truly the way of life with God is submission to the One God, and at variance were those who were given the Book after what had drawn near to them of knowledge out of insolence among themselves, and whoever is ungrateful for the signs of God, then truly God is Swift in reckoning.

(3:26) Say: O God! The One Who is Sovereign of Dominion, Thou givest dominion to whom Thou wilt and Thou tearest away dominion from whom Thou wilt and Thou renderest powerful whom Thou wilt and Thou abasest whom Thou wilt; in Thy hand is the good; truly Thou art Powerful over everything. (3:27) Thou causest the nighttime to be interposed into the daytime, and Thou causest the daytime to be interposed into the nighttime; and Thou bringest out the living from the dead and Thou bringest out the dead from the living; and Thou providest to whomever Thou wilt without stinting.

(3:73) And believe none but one who has heeded your way of life. Say: Truly guidance is The Guidance from God and believe not that anyone be given the like of what you were given so that he may argue with you before your Lord, say: Truly the grace is in the hand of God. He gives it to whomever He wills, and God is One Who Embraces, Knowing. (3:74) He singles out for His mercy whom He wills, and God is Possessor of Sublime Grace.

(3:189) To God belongs the dominion of the heavens and of the earth, and God is Powerful over everything. (3:190) Truly in the creation of the heavens and of the earth and the alteration of nighttime and daytime, there are signs for those who have intuition, (3:191) those who remember God while upright and sitting and on their sides and they reflect on the creation of the heavens and the earth. Our Lord! Thou hast not created this in vain. Glory be to Thee! Then protect us from the punishment of the fire. (3:192) Our Lord! Whomever Thou causest to enter the fire, surely Thou hast covered him with shame; and there will not be for the ones who are unjust any helpers.

Chapter 4: Women 2 Signs

(4:171) O People of the Book! Go not beyond the limits in your way of life and say not about God but The Truth: That the Messiah, Jesus son of Mary, was a Messenger of God and His word that He cast to Mary and a Spirit from Him; so believe in God and His Messengers; and say not: Three. To refrain yourselves from it is better for you. There is only One God; glory be to Him that He should have a son! To Him belongs whatever is in the heavens and whatever is in and on the earth, and God has sufficed as a Trustee. (4:172) The Messiah will never disdain that he be a servant of God, nor the angels, ones who are brought near to Him. And whoever disdains His worship and grows arrogant, He will assemble them altogether to Himself.

Chapter 5 The Table Spread With Food 10 Signs

(5:17) Certainly ungrateful are those who said: Truly God is the Messiah, the son of Mary. Say: Who then has any sway against God? If He wanted to He would have caused to perish the Messiah son of Mary and his mother, and whatever is in and on the earth altogether, to God belongs the dominion of the heavens and the earth and what is between the two. He creates what He wills. And God is Powerful over everything.

(5:40) Knowest thou not that to God, to Him belongs the dominion of the heavens and the earth? He punishes whom He wills and He forgives whom He wills, and God is Powerful over everything.

(5:97) God has made the Kabah the Sacred House, maintaining it for humanity and the Sacred Month and the sacrificial gift and the garlanded. That is so that you will know that God knows whatever is in the heavens and whatever is in and on the earth and that God is Knowing of everything. (5:98) Know that God is Severe in repayment and that God is Forgiving, Compassionate. (5:99) What is with the Messenger is not but the delivery of the message, and God knows whatever you show and whatever you keep back.

(5:116) And mention when God said: O Jesus son of Mary! Hast thou said to humanity: Take me and my mother to yourselves other than God; He would say: Glory be to Thee! It was not for me that I say what I have no right to say. If I had said it then surely Thou wouldst have known it.

Thou knowest what is in my soul and I know not what is in Thy Soul. Truly Thou, Thou art Knower of the unseen. (5:117) I said not to them but what Thou hast commanded me of it: That you worship God, my Lord and your Lord. And I was witness for them so long as I stood persistently among them; then when Thou hast gathered me to Thyself, Thou wert Thyself The Watcher over them. Thou art truly Witness over everything. (5:118) If Thou wert to punish them, then they are but Thy servants; and if Thou wert to forgive them truly Thou, Thou art The Almighty, The Wise. (5:119) God would say: This Day the ones who are sincere will profit from their sincerity. For them are Gardens beneath which rivers run, ones who will dwell in them forever, eternally. God is well-pleased with them and they are well-pleased with Him. That is the winning the sublime triumph. (5:120) To God belongs the dominion of the heavens and the earth and whatever is in and on them. And He is Powerful over everything.

Chapter 6 The Flocks 45 Signs

(6:1) The Praise belongs to God Who created the heavens and the earth and made the shadows and the light; after that those who are ungrateful to their Lord, they equate others to Him. (6:2) It is He Who created you from clay, and after that decided a term; a term, that which was determined by Him; after that you contest. (6:3) And He is God in the heavens and in and on the earth; He knows your secret and what you openly publish and He knows whatever you earn.

(6:13) And to Him belongs whatever inhabits the nighttime and the daytime. And He is The Hearing, The Knowing. (6:14) Say: Will I take to myself, other than God, a protector, One Who is Originator of the heavens and the earth? And it is He who feeds and He who is never fed, say: Truly I was commanded that I be the first who is submitting to the One

God; and be thou not among the ones who are polytheists. (6:15) Say: Truly I fear if I rebel against my Lord, the punishment of the tremendous Day! (6:16) He who is turned away from it on that Day, then surely He had mercy on him. And that is the winning the clear triumph. (6:17) And if God touches you with distress, then no one will remove it but He; and if He touches you with good, then He is Powerful over everything. (6:18) He is The One Who is Omniscient over His servants. And He is the The Wise, The Aware.

(6:38) And there is no moving creature in or on the earth, no fowl that flies with its two wings but they are communities like yours. We have not neglected anything in the Book. After that they will be assembled to their Lord.

(6:46) Say: Have you yourself considered if God took your ability to hear and your sight and set a seal on your hearts, what god other than God would restore them to you, look on how We diversify the signs. After that they still draw aside. (6:47) Say: Have you yourself considered if the punishment of God approached you suddenly or publicly, will anyone be caused to perish but the folk, the ones who are unjust?

(6:59) With Him are the keys of the unseen. None knows them but He. And He knows whatever is on dry land and in the sea. Not a leaf descends but He knows it nor a grain in the shadows of the earth nor fresh nor dry thing but it is in a clear Book. (6:60) It is He Who gathers you to Himself by nighttime and He knows what you are busy with by daytime. After that He raises you up in it so that the term, that which was determined, is decided; after that to Him is your return. Then He will tell you of what you had been doing. (6:61) And He is The One Who Is Omniscient over His servants; and He sends over you recorders until when death draws near to anyone of you. Our messengers gather him to themselves and they neglect not. (6:62) After that they would be returned to God, their Defender, The True. Is not the determination for Him? And He is The Swiftest of the ones who reckon. (6:63) Say: Who delivers you from the shadows of the dry land and the sea? You call to Him humbly and inwardly: If He rescues us from this, we will be of the ones who are thankful. (6:64) Say: God delivers you from them and from every distress. After that you ascribe partners to Him. (6:65) Say: He is One Who Has Power to raise up on you a punishment from above you or from beneath your feet or to confuse you as partisans and to cause you to experience the violence of some of you to one another, look at how We diversify the signs so that perhaps they would understand!

(6:73) And it is He Who created the heavens and the earth with The Truth; and on a Day He says: Be! Then it is! His saying is The Truth. And His is the kingship on a Day when the trumpet will be blown. He is One Who Has Knowledge of the unseen and the visible. And He is The Wise, The Aware. (6:74) And when Abraham said to his father Azar: Takest thou idols to thyself as gods? Truly I see thee and thy folk clearly wandering astray. (6:75) And thus We caused Abraham to see the kingdom of the heavens and the earth so that he would be of the ones who are certain in belief. (6:76) So when night outspread over him, he saw a star; he said: This is my Lord; then when it set, he said: I love not that which sets. (6:77) Then when he saw the moon, that which rises, he said: This is my Lord; then when it set, he said: If my Lord guides me not, I will certainly have been among the folk, ones gone astray. (6:78) Then when he saw the sun, that which rises, he said: This is my Lord; this is greater; then when it set, he said: O my folk! Truly I am free from the partners you ascribe to Him. (6:79) Truly I have turned my face to He Who Originated the heavens and the earth—as a monotheist; and I am not of the ones who are polytheists.

(6:95) Truly it is God who is One Who Causes to Break Forth the grain and the pit of a date; He brings out the living from the dead and is One Who Brings Forth the dead from the living. That is God; then how you are mislead. (6:96) He is One Who Causes to Break Forth the morning dawn and He has made the night as a place of rest and the sun and the moon to keep count. That is the decree of The Almighty, The Knowing. (6:97) And it is He Who has made the stars for you so that you will be truly guided by them in the shadows of dry land and the sea, surely We have explained distinctly the signs for a folk who know. (6:98) And it is He Who caused you to grow from a single soul, then a temporary stay and a repository, surely We have explained distinctly the signs for a folk who understand. (6:99) And it is He Who sends forth water from heaven. Then We brought out from it every kind of bringing forth. Then We brought out herbs from it. We brought out from it thick-clustered grain and from the date palm tree, from the spathe of it, thick clusters of dates, ones that are drawn near and gardens of the grapevines and the olives and the pomegranates resembling and not resembling one another, look on its fruit when it bears fruit and its ripening. Truly in this are signs for a folk who believe. (6:100) And they made as associates with God the jinn although He created them; and they falsely attributed to Him sons and daughters without knowledge. Glory be to Him! Exalted is He above what they allege. (6:101) He is Originator of the heavens and the earth; how would He have a child when He has had no companion; and He has created everything; and He is Knowing of everything? (6:102) That is God, your Lord; there is no god but He; the One Who is Creator of everything so worship Him. For He is Trustee over everything. (6:103) No sight apprehends Him but He apprehends sight; and He is The Subtle, The Aware. (6:104) Surely clear evidence has drawn near to you from your Lord; so whoever perceives, it is for his own soul; whoever is in darkness, it is against his own soul. Say: And I am not a guardian over you.

(6:115) The Word of thy Lord has been completed in sincerity and justice. There is no one who changes His Words. And He is the The Hearing, The Knowing.

(6:133) Thy Lord is The Sufficient, Possessor of Mercy. If He wills, He will cause you to be put away and will make a successor after you of whomever He wills, just as He caused you to grow from offspring of other folk.

(6:141) And it is He Who caused gardens to grow, with trellises and without trellises and the date palm trees and a variety of harvest crops and the olives and the pomegranates resembling and not resembling one another. Eat of its fruit when it bears fruit and give its due on the day of its reaping; and exceed not all bounds. Truly God loves not the ones who are excessive. (6:142) And of the flocks are some as beasts of burden and some for slaughter. Eat of what God has provided you and follow not in the steps of Satan. Truly he is a clear enemy to you.

(6:162) Say: Truly my formal prayer, and my ritual sacrifice and my living and my dying are for God, Lord of all the worlds. (6:163) He has no associate and of this was I commanded and I am the first of the ones who submit. (6:164) Say: Is it other than God that I should desire as a lord while He is Lord of everything? And each soul will earn only for itself. No soul laden will bear another's heavy load. After that to your Lord will you return. Then He will tell you about what you had been at variance in it. (6:165) And it is He who has made you as viceregents on the earth and has exalted some of you above others in degree that He might try you with what He has given you, truly thy Lord is Swift in repayment and He truly is Forgiving, Compassionate.

Chapter 7 The Elevated Places 10 Signs

(7:10) And certainly We established you firmly on the earth and We made for you in it a livelihood, but little you give thanks. (7:11) And certainly We created you, after that formed you. After that We said to the angels: Prostrate before Adam! Then they prostrated but Iblis. He is not of the ones who prostrated.

(7:43) . . . . and they will say: The Praise belongs to God Who has truly guided us to this! And we would not have been guided if God had not guided us; certainly the Messengers of our Lord drew near us with The Truth; and it will be proclaimed to them that this is the Garden to be given to you as inheritance for what you had been doing.

(7:54) Truly your Lord is God, He Who created the heavens and the earth in six days. After that He turned His attention to the Throne. He covers the nighttime with the daytime which seeks it out urgently and the sun and the moon and the stars are ones that were caused to be subservient to His command, truly His is not but the creation and the command, blessed be God, Lord of the worlds. (7:55) Call to your Lord humbly and inwardly. Truly He loves not the ones who are aggressors. (7:56) Make not corruption in the earth after things have been made right and call to Him with fear and hope. Truly the mercy of God is Near to the ones who are doers of good. (7:57) And it is He Who sends the winds, ones that are bearers of good tidings of His mercy; until when they are charged with a heavy cloud, We will drive it to a dead land and then We send forth water from the cloud and with it We bring out by water every kind of fruit. Thus We will bring out the dead so that perhaps you would recollect. (7:58) As for the good land, its plants go forth with permission of its Lord; while, as for what is bad, it goes forth not but scantily. Thus We diversify the signs for a folk who give thanks.

(7:143) And when Moses drew near Our time appointed and his Lord spoke to him, he said: O my Lord! Cause me to see that I may look on Thee. He said: Thou shalt never see

Me but look on the mountain. Then if it stays fast in its place, thou might see Me. Then when his Lord Self-disclosed to the mountain, He made it as ground powder and Moses fell down swooning. And when he recovered he said: Glory be to Thee! I repent to Thee and I am the first one who believes.

(7:185) Have they not expected in the kingship of the heavens and the earth and whatever things God has created that perhaps their term has neared; then in what discourse after this will they believe?

Chapter 9 Repentance 4 Signs

(9:31) They have taken to themselves their learned Jewish scholars and their monks as lords other than God and the Messiah son of Mary. And they were only commanded to worship The One God; there is no god but He! Glory be to Him from the partners they make! (9:32) They want to extinguish the light of God with their mouths, but God refuses so that He may fulfill His light even though the ones who are ungrateful dislike it. (9:33) It is He Who has sent His Messenger with the guidance and the way of life of The Truth so that He will uplift it over all ways of life, even though the ones who are polytheists dislike it.

(9:116) Truly, God, to Him belongs the dominion of the heavens and the earth; He gives life and He causes death. And there is not for you other than God, either a protector nor a helper.

Chapter 10 Jonah 18 Signs

(10:3) Truly your Lord is God Who created the heavens and the earth in six days, after that turned Himself to the Throne; managing the command; there is no intercessor but after His permission. That is God, your Lord, so worship Him alone. Will you not then recollect? (10:4) To Him is your return, all; the promise of God is true. (10:5) It is He Who begins the creation. After that He will cause it to return so that He may give recompense to those who have believed and the ones who have acted in accord with morality with equity. And those who are ungrateful, for them is a drink of boiling water and a painful punishment because they had been ungrateful. It is He Who made the sun an illumination and the moon as a light and ordained its phases so that you would know the number of the years and the reckoning. God created that only in Truth. He explains distinctly the signs for a folk who know. (10:6) Truly in the alternation of the nighttime and the daytime and all that God has created in the heavens and the earth are signs for a folk who are Godfearing.

(10:31) Say: Who provides for you from the heaven and the earth? Who controls having the ability to hear and sight? And Who brings out the living from the dead and brings out the dead from the living? And who manages the command? They will then say: God! Say: Will you not be Godfearing? (10:32) Such is God, your Lord, The Truth; and what else is there after The Truth but wandering astray; how then are you turned away?

(10:61) Neither hast thou been on any matter nor hast thou been recounting from the Recitation nor have you been doing any action but We have been ones who bear witness over you when you have been pressing on it. And nothing escapes from thy Lord of the weight of an atom in or on the earth nor in the heaven nor what is smaller than that nor what is greater than that, but it is in a clear Book.

(10:67) It is He Who has made the nighttime for you so that you may rest in it and the daytime for one who perceives. Truly in this are signs for a folk who hear. (10:68) They say God has taken to Himself a son, glory be to Him; He is Sufficient; To Him is whatever is in the heavens and in and on the earth. You have no authority for this. Say you against God what you know not?

(10:99) And had thy Lord willed, all of those on earth would have believed. So wouldst thou compel humanity against their will until they become ones who believe? (10:100) And it would not be for any person to believe but by the permission of God. And He will disgrace those who are not reasonable. (10:101) Say: Look upon what is in the heavens and the earth. And neither the signs nor the warning avail a folk who believe not.

(10:104) Say: O humanity! If you are in uncertainty as to my way of life, then I will not worship those whom you worship other than God, but I worship only God. Who will call you to Himself; and I was commanded to be among ones who believe (10:105) and that thou set thy face to the way of life of a monotheist and never be among the ones who are polytheists. (10:106) And call not to other than God what can neither profit nor harm thee; and if thou wert to accomplish that, truly thou wouldst be among the ones who are unjust. (10:107) And if God afflicts thee with an injury, there is no one who removes it but He; and if He wants good for thee, there is no one who repels His grace. It lights on whomever He wills of His servants and He is The Forgiving, The Compassionate. (10:108) Say: O humanity! Surely The Truth has drawn near to you from your Lord; so whoever is truly guided, then he is only truly guided for his own soul; and whoever goes astray, then he only strays to his own loss; and I am not a trustee over you. (10:109) And follow what is revealed to thee and have patience until God gives judgment. And He is the Best of the ones who judge.

Chapter 11 Hud 11 Signs

(11:4) To God is your return; and He is Powerful over everything. (11:5) But they fold up their breasts that they may conceal themselves from Him. No doubt at the time when they cover themselves with their garments, He knows what they keep secret and what they speak openly. Truly He is the Knowing of what is in their breasts. (11:6) And there is no moving creature on earth but its provision is due from God and He knows its appointed time and its repository. All is in a clear Book.

(11:44) And it was said: O earth! Take in your water! And O heaven: Desist! And the water shrank and the command of God was satisfied and it was on the same level as Al-Judi; and it was said: Away with the folk, the ones who are unjust!

(11:56) Truly I have put my trust in God, my Lord and your Lord. There is not a moving creature but He is the One Who Takes of its forelock. Truly my Lord is on a straight path. (11:57) But if you turn away, that is your decision. Then surely I have expressed to you what I was sent with to you. And my Lord will make successors a folk other than you and you will not injure Him at all. Truly My Lord is Guardian over everything.

(11:118) And had thy Lord willed, He would have made humanity one community; but they continue to be ones who are at variance (11:119) except on whom thy Lord has bestowed His mercy. And for that, He created them, and the Word of thy Lord has been completed. Certainly I will fill hell with genie and humanity altogether. (11:120) And all that We relate to thee of the tidings of the Messengers is so that We make thy mind firm by it. And The Truth has drawn near to thee in this, and an admonishment and a reminder for the ones who believe. (11:121) And say to those who believe not: Act according to your ability. Truly We are ones who act. (11:122) And watch and wait. We too are ones who are watching and waiting. (11:123) And to God belongs the unseen of the heavens and the earth and to Him is the return of the command so worship Him and put thy trust in Him. And thy Lord is not One Who is Heedless of what you do.

Chapter 13 Thunder 19 Signs

(13:1) *Alif Lām Mīm Rā*. These are the signs of the Book, and what were sent forth to thee from thy Lord is The Truth but most of humanity believes not. (13:2) It is He Who exalted the heavens without any pillars so that you see them; then He turned his attention to above the Throne; and He caused to become subservient the sun and the moon; each running for a term; that which was determined. He manages the command. He explains distinctly the signs so that perhaps of the meeting with your Lord you would be certain. (13:3) And it is He Who stretched out the earth and made on it firm mountains and rivers; and with every kind of fruit. He made in it two mates. He covers the nighttime with the daytime. Truly in that are signs for a folk who reflect. (13:4) And in the earth there are strips those which neighbor one another and gardens of grapevines and plowed lands and date palm trees coming from the same root and not coming from the same root that are watered with one water and We have some preferred some of them over others in produce. Truly in these things there are signs for a folk who are reasonable.

(13:8) God knows what every female carries and how much her womb absorbs and what they add; and everything with Him is in proportion. (13:9) He is One Who Has Knowledge of the unseen and the visible, The Great, One Who is Exalted. (13:10) It is the same to Him whether you be one who keeps secret his saying or one who publishes it or whoever he be, one who conceals himself by nighttime or one who goes about carelessly in the daytime. (13:11) For him there are the ones who postpone from before him and from behind him keeping him safe by the command of God, truly God alters not a folk until they alter what is within themselves, and when God wants evil for a folk, then there is no averting it. And there is not for them other than He any one who is a safeguarder. (13:12) It is He Who causes you to see the lightning in fear and in hope. And it is He Who causes the clouds to grow heavy. (13:13) And thunder glorifies His praise and the angels because of their awe of Him. And He sends thunderbolts and He lights on whom He wills. And they dispute about God, and He is a Severe Force. (13:14) For Him is the call of The Truth; and those whom they call to other than Him, they respond not to them at all but like one who stretches out the palms of his hands for water so that it should reach his mouth, but it carries not through. And supplication of the ones who are ungrateful is not but to wander astray. (13:15) And to God prostrates whoever is in the heavens and the earth, willingly or unwillingly, and their shade in the first part of the day and at eventide. (13:16) Say: Who is the Lord of the heavens and the earth? Say: God! Say: Have you taken other than Him to yourself as protectors? They have no control over themselves, neither profiting nor hurting. Say: Are the unwilling to see on the same level as the willingly seeing? Are the shadows on the same level as the light, ascribe they associates with God who have created as He created so that creation seems alike to them? Say: God is the Creator of everything and He is The One, The Omniscient. (13:17) He sends forth water from heaven and it flows into valleys according to their measure then the flood bears away the swelling froth. And from what they kindle in a fire, looking for glitter or sustenance, there is a froth the like of it. Thus God compares The Truth and falsehood. Then as for the froth, it goes as swelling scum; while what profits humanity abides on the earth. Thus God propounds parables. (13:18) Ruby and Pearl: For those who respond to their Lord there is the fairest. And for those who respond not to Him, if they had all that is in and on the earth and its like with it, they would offer it as ransom. Those, for them will be a dire reckoning and their place of shelter will be hell. How miserable it is as cradling!

(13:38) And certainly We sent Messengers before thee and We assigned for them spouses and offspring. And it had not been for a Messenger to bring a sign but with the permission of God, for each and every term there is a Book. (13:39) God blots out what He wills and brings to a stand still what He wills; and with Him is the essence of the Book. (13:40) And whether We cause thee to see some of what We have promised them or call thee to Ourself, thy duty is delivering the message and on Us is the reckoning. (13:41) Have they not considered that We approach the earth, reducing it from its outlying parts? And God gives judgment. There is no one who postpones His determination. And He is Swift in reckoning. (13:42) And surely those who were before them planned, so to God is the plan altogether; He knows what every person earns, and the ones who are ungrateful will know for whom will be the Ultimate Abode. (13:43) And those who are ungrateful say: Thou art not one who is sent. Say: God has sufficed as a witness between me and between you and whoever has knowledge of the Book.

Chapter 14 Abraham 9 Signs

(14:1) *Alif Lām Rā*. This is a Book We have sent forth to thee so that thou mayest bring humanity out from the shadows into the light with the permission of their Lord to the path of The Almighty, The Worthy of Praise. (14:2) God! To Him belongs all that is in the heavens and all that is in and on the earth, and woe to the ones who are ungrateful. For them is the severe punishment,

(14:32) God is He Who has created the heavens and the earth and sent forth water from heaven and brought out thereby fruit as provision for you; and causes boats to become subservient to you that they may run through the sea by His command; and He causes rivers to become subservient to you. (14:33) And He caused the sun to be subservient to you and the moon, both constant in their work; and He caused the nighttime to be subservient to you and the daytime. (14:34) And He gave you all that you asked of Him. And if you were to number the divine blessing of God, you would not count them, truly the human being is wrongdoing and an ingrate.

(14:48) On a day when the earth will be substituted for other than this earth and the heavens; they will depart to God, The One, The Omniscient God. (14:49) And thou shalt consider the ones who sin that Day, ones who were bound in chains. (14:50) Their tunics are made of pitch and the fire will overcome their faces (14:51) so that God may give recompense to each soul for what it has earned. Truly God is Swift in reckoning. (14:52) This is the delivering of the message to humanity so that they may be warned by it and that they may know that He is One God so that those who have intuition may recollect.

Chapter 15 The Rocky Tract 9 Signs

(15:19) And We stretched out the earth and cast on it firm mountains and caused to develop on it that which was well-balanced of each thing. (15:20) And We made on it for you a livelihood and for those whom you are not ones who provide. (15:21) And there is not a thing but its treasures are with Us and We send down not but in a known measure.

(15:22) And We send fertilizing winds. Then We send forth water from heaven, satiating you, and you are not ones who are its treasurers. (15:23) And truly it is We Who give life and cause to die and We are the ones who inherit. (15:24) And certainly We know the ones of you who came first and certainly We know the ones who come later. (15:25) And truly thy Lord is He Who assembles. Truly He is Wise, Knowing. (15:26) And certainly We created the human being from clay of molded mud. (15:27) And We created the spirits before from the fire of a pestilential wind.

Chapter 16 The Bee 49 Signs

(16:1) The command of God is approaching. Seek not to hasten it. Glory be to Him and exalted is He above all the partners they make with Him. (16:2) He sends down the angels with the Spirit of His command to whom He will of His servants to warn that there is no god but I, so be Godfearing of Me. (16:3) He has created the heavens and the earth with The Truth. He is to be exalted above all partners they make with Him. (16:4) He created the human being from a seminal fluid. Lo and behold! He is a clear adversary. (16:5) And He has created the flocks, for you in which there is warmth and many uses and of them you eat (16:6) and in them is a beauty for you when you give them rest and when you drive forth flocks to pasture. (16:7) And they carry your lading to a land, one you would not reach but under adverse circumstances to yourselves. Truly your Lord is Gentle, Compassionate. (16:8) And He has created horses, mules and donkeys, for you to ride and as an adornment. And He creates what you know not. (16:9) And with God is the showing of the way yet some of them are ones who swerve. And had He willed, He would have guided you all. (16:10) It is He Who sends forth water from heaven; for you from it to drink and from it, trees wherein you pasture your herds. (16:11) He causes crops to develop for you with it, and the olives and the date palms and the grapevines, and from every kind of fruit, truly in that is a sign for a folk who reflect. (16:12) And He causes to become subservient to you the nighttime and the daytime and the sun and the moon; and the stars, subservient by His command, truly in that are signs for a folk, who are reasonable. (16:13) And whatever He made numerous for you in and on the earth of hues, ones that are at variance truly in that is a sign for a folk who recollect. (16:14) And He it is

Who has caused the sea to become subservient to you so that you eat from it succulent flesh and pull out of it glitter to wear. And you see the ships, ones that plow through the waves, that you may be looking for His grace and so that perhaps you would be thankful. (16:15) And He cast on to the earth firm mountains so that it not vibrate with you and rivers and roads so that perhaps you would be truly guided (16:16) and landmarks. And they are truly guided by the stars. (16:17) Is then He Who creates as one who creates not, will you then not recollect? (16:18) And if you try to count the divine blessing of God, you will not be able to count it, truly God is Forgiving, Compassionate. (16:19) And God knows what you keep secret and what you speak openly. (16:20) And those whom you call to other than God, they create not anything but they are themselves created. (16:21) They are lifeless, not living; and they are not aware when they will be raised up. (16:22) Your God is One God. But for those who believe not in the world to come, their hearts are ones that know not and they are ones who grow arrogant. (16:23) Without a doubt God knows what they keep secret, and what they speak openly. Truly He loves not the ones who grow in arrogance.

(16:48) Consider they not that whatever things God has created casts its shadow to the right and to the left, ones who prostrate to God, and they are ones who are in a state of lowliness? (16:49) And to God prostrates whatever is in the heavens and whatever is in and on the earth of moving creatures and the angels and they grow not arrogant. (16:51) And God said: Take not two gods to yourselves; truly He is One God; then have reverence for Me. (16:52) And to Him belongs all that is in the heavens and the earth and His is the way of life forever. Are you Godfearing of other than God? (16:53) And whatever you have of divine blessing is from God; after that when injury afflicts you, you make entreaties to Him. (16:54) After that when He has removed the injury from you, lo and behold! A group of people among you make partners with their Lord. (16:55) They are ungrateful for what We have given them. So let them take joy; soon they will know.

(16:65) And God sent forth water from heaven and from it gave life to the earth after its death. Truly in this is a sign for a folk who hear. (16:66) And truly for you in the flocks is a lesson; We satiate you from what is in their bellies —from between waste and blood— exclusively milk, that which is delicious to the ones who drink. (16:67) From fruits of the date palm trees and grapevines you take to yourself of it an intoxicant and fair provisions, truly in it is a sign for a folk who are reasonable. (16:68) And thy Lord reveals to the bee: Take to thyself houses from the mountains and in the trees and in what they construct. (16:69) Then eat of all fruits and insert thyself submissively into the ways of thy Lord. Drink goes forth from their bellies in hues, ones that are at variance, wherein is healing for humanity, truly in this is certainly a sign for a folk who reflect. (16:70) And God has created you. Then He calls you to Himself. And of you there are some who are returned to the vilest of lifetimes so that he knows nothing after having known something. Truly God is Knowing, Powerful. (16:71) And God gave advantage to some of you above others in provisions. But those who were given advantage are not ones who give over wealth to what their right hands possess so that they are equal in it. Why have they negated the divine blessing of God? (16:72) And God has assigned to you mates of your own kind and has assigned you from your mates, children and grandchildren and has provided you with what is good. They believe then in falsehood and are ungrateful for the divine blessing of God?

(16:77) And to God is the unseen of the heavens and the earth. And the command of the Hour is not but the twinkling of an eye to one's sight or it is nearer. Truly God is Powerful over everything. (16:78) And God brought you out from the wombs of your mothers and you knew nothing. And He assigned to you the ability to hear and sight and mind so that perhaps you would be thankful. (16:79) Have you not considered the birds, the ones who are subservient in the firmament of the heavens? None holds them back but God, truly in this are the signs for a folk who believe. (16:80) And God has assigned for you your houses as places of rest and assigned for you the hides of flocks for houses which you find light on the day of your departing and the day of your halting and of their wool and fur and hair, furnishings and enjoyment for a while. (16:81) And God has made for you shade out of what He created and has made for you the mountains as a refuge in the time of need and has made for you tunics to protect you from the heat and tunics to protect you from your violence. Thus He fulfills His divine blessing to you so that perhaps you would submit.

(16:93) Had God willed, He would have made you all one community, but He causes to go astray whom He wills and guides whom He wills. And certainly you will be asked about what you had been doing.

Chapter 17 The Journey by Night 9 Signs

(17:12) We have made the nighttime and the daytime as two signs; then We blotted out the sign of nighttime and We made the sign of daytime for one who perceives that you may look for grace from your Lord and that you may know the number of years and the reckoning. And We have explained everything distinctly, with a decisive explanation. (17:13) For each human being We have fastened his omen to his neck and We will bring out for him on the Day of Resurrection a book in which he will meet that which had unfolded. (17:14) Recite thy book! This day thy soul has sufficed against thee as thy reckoner. (17:15) Whoever is truly guided is guided only for his own soul; and whoever goes astray, then only goes astray against it. And no one bears the heavy load of another, nor would We be ones who punish until We have raised up a Messenger.

(17:42) Say: If there had been gods along with Him as they say, then they would have certainly been looking for a way to the Lord of the Throne. (17:43) Glory be to Him! And exalted is He above what they say, greatly exalted. (17:44) The seven heavens glorify Him and the earth and all that is in and on them. There is not a thing but it glorifies His praise, but you understand not their glorification, truly He has been Forbearing, Forgiving.

(17:70) And certainly We held the Children of Adam in esteem and We carried them on dry land and on the sea and have provided them with what is good and We have preferred them over many of those whom We created with excellence.

(17:111) And say: The Praise belongs to God Who has taken neither a son to Himself and there is not for Him an associate in the dominion nor is there for Him need for a protector out of humility; and magnify Him a magnification!

Chapter 19 Mary 3 Signs

(19:93) There is none at all in the heavens and the earth but he be one who arrives to The Merciful as a servant. (19:94) Certainly He has counted them and summed up a number! (19:95) And everyone of them will be ones who arrive to Him individually on the Day of Resurrection.

Chapter 20 TaHa 9 Signs

(20:1) Ṭā Hā. (20:2) We have not sent forth the Quran to thee that thou shouldst be unhappy, (20:3) but as an admonition to him who dreads; (20:4) a sending down successively from Him Who has created the earth and the lofty heavens. (20:5) The Merciful turned His attention to the Throne. (20:6) To Him belongs whatever is in the heavens and whatever is on the earth and whatever is between them and whatever is under the soil. (20:7) And if thou wert to publish a saying, yet truly He knows the secret and what is even more hidden. (20:8) God, there is no god but He; to Him belong the Fairest Names.

(20:49) He said: Then who is the Lord of you two, O Moses? (20:50) He said: Our Lord is He Who gave each thing its creation then He guided it. (20:51) Pharaoh said: Then what of the first generations? (20:52) Moses said: That knowledge is with my Lord in a Book; my Lord neither goes astray nor forgets. (20:53) He Who assigned for you the earth as a cradle and threaded ways for you in it and sent forth water from heaven and We brought out from it diverse pairs of plants: (20:54) Eat and pasture your flocks, truly in this are signs for the people who have sense. (20:55) We created you from it and into it We will cause you to return and from it We will bring you out a time again. (20:56) And certainly We caused him to see Our signs —all of them— but he denied and refused.

(20:108) On that Day they will follow one who calls. There will be no crookedness in him; and voices will be hushed for The Merciful so thou shalt hear nothing but a murmuring. (20:109) On that Day intercession will not profit anyone but such as one to whom permission has been given by The Merciful and with whose saying He is well-pleased. (20:110) He knows what is in advance of them, and what is behind them and they will not comprehend Him in their knowledge. (20:111) And faces will be humbled before The Living, The Eternal; while surely will be frustrated whoever is burdened by doing injustice.

Chapter 21 The Prophets 21 Signs

(21:16) And We created not the heavens and the earth and what is between them as ones in play. (21:17) Had We wanted We would have taken some diversion. We would have taken it to Ourselves from that which proceeds from Our Presence if We had been ones who do so. (21:18) Nay! We hurl The Truth against falsehood so it prevails over it. Then lo and behold! Falsehood is that which vanishes. And woe to you for what you allege. (21:19) And to Him belongs whoever is in the heavens and the earth. And those who are near Him. They grow not arrogant to worship Him nor they become weary. (21:20) They glorify Him nighttime and daytime. They never decrease. (21:21) Or have they taken gods to themselves from the earth, they, ones who revive the dead? (21:22) Had there been gods in it—other than God— certainly both would have gone to ruin. Then glory be to God! Lord of the Throne! High above what they allege. (21:23) He will not be asked as to what He accomplished but they will be asked. (21:24) Or have they taken gods to themselves other than He; say: Prepare your proof; this is a Remembrance such a one who is with me and a Remembrance for those who were before me, nay! Most of them know not The Truth; so they are ones who turn aside. (21:25) And We sent not before thee any Messenger, but We revealed to him that there is no god but I, so worship Me. (21:26) And they say: The Merciful has taken to Himself a son, glory be to Him! Nay! They were honored servants! (21:27) They precede Him not in saying and they act by His command. (21:28) He knows what is in advance of them and what is behind them and they intercede not but for him with whom He is content. And they, from being apprehensive of Him, are ones in dread. (21:29) And whoever says of them: Truly I am a god other than He. Then We will give recompense to him with hell. Thus We give recompense to the ones who are unjust. (21:30) Have not those who are ungrateful not considered that the heavens and the earth had been interwoven and We unstitched them; and We have made every living thing of water; will they then not believe? (21:31) And We have made firm mountains on the earth so that it should not vibrate with them and We made in it ravines as ways so that perhaps they would be truly guided. (21:32) And We have made heaven as a guarded roof; yet they are ones who turn aside from its signs. (21:33) And it is He Who has created the nighttime and the daytime the sun and the moon; each swimming in orbit. (21:34) And We assigned not to any mortal before thee immortality; If thou wert to die will they be ones who dwell forever? (21:35) Every soul will be one that experiences death, and We will try you with a chastisement and good as a test; and to Us you will be returned.

Chapter 22 The Pilgrimage 16 Signs

(22:1) O humanity! Be Godfearing of your Lord. Truly the earthquake of the Hour is a tremendous thing. (22:2) On a Day you will see it. Every one who is suckling will be negligent of whoever she suckled. And every pregnant woman will bring forth a foetus and thou shalt see humanity as intoxicated yet they will not be intoxicated. But the punishment of God will be severe. (22:3) And among humanity is he who disputes about God without knowledge and follows every rebel satan. (22:4) It was written down about him that whoever turns away, truly he will cause him to go astray and will guide him to the punishment of the Blaze. (22:5) O humanity! If you have been in doubt about the Uprising, truly We created you from earth dust and after that from seminal fluids and after that from a clot and after that from tissue that was formed and that was not formed so that we may make it manifest to you. We establish in the wombs whom We will for a term, that which was determined. and after that

We bring you out as infant children and after that you may reach the coming of age; and among you there is he whom death calls to itself, and among you there is he who is returned to the vilest lifetime so that he knows not anything after some knowledge. And you see the earth lifeless. Yet when We send forth water on it, it quivers and it swells and puts forth every lovely pair. (22:6) That is because God, He is The Truth, and it is He Who gives life to the dead and He is Powerful over everything. (22:7) And truly the Hour is one that arrives. There is no doubt about it and that God will raise up those who are in the graves.

(22:18) Hast thou not considered that to God prostrates to Him whoever is in the heavens and whoever is in and on the earth and the sun and the moon and the stars, the mountains, the trees and the moving creatures, and many of humanity; many on whom the punishment will be realized, and He whom God despises, then there is none who honors him. Truly God accomplishes whatever He wills.

(22:61) That is because God causes the nighttime to be inserted into the daytime and He causes the daytime to be inserted into the nighttime. And truly God is Hearing, Seeing. (22:62) That is because God, He is The Truth and that what they call to other than Him, it is falsehood and that God, He is The Lofty, The Great. (22:63) Hast thou not considered that God sends forth water from heaven and the earth becomes green, truly God is Subtle, Aware. (22:64) To Him belongs whatever is in the heavens and whatever is in and on the earth, and truly God, He is The Sufficient, The Worthy of Praise. (22:65) Hast thou not considered that God has caused to be subservient to you what is in and on the earth. And the boats run through the sea by His command and He holds back the heaven so that it not fall on the earth, but by His permission, truly to humanity God is Gentle, Compassionate. (22:66) And it is He Who gave you life. and after that He will cause you to die and after that He will give you life again, truly the human being is ungrateful.

(22:70) Knowest thou not that God knows what is in the heaven and the earth, truly that is in a Book. Truly that is easy for God.

(22:73) O humanity! A parable was propounded, so listen to it. Truly those whom you call to other than God will never create a fly, even though they be gathered together for it; and if the fly were to rob them of something, they would never seek to deliver it from the fly. Weak are the ones who are seekers and the ones who were sought. (22:74) They have not duly measured the measure of God, truly God is Strong, Almighty. (22:75) God favors from the angels messengers and from humanity. Truly God is Hearing, Seeing. (22:76) He knows what is in advance of them, and what is behind them, and to God all affairs return.

Chapter 23 The Believers 29 Signs
(23:12) And certainly We have created the human being from an extraction of clay. (23:13) After that We made him into seminal fluid in a stopping place, secure. (23:14) After that We created a clot from seminal fluids. Then We created tissue from the clot. Then We created bones from tissue. Then We clothed the bones with flesh. After that We caused another creation to grow. So blessed be God, the Fairest of Creators! (23:15) After that truly you will die. (23:16) After that truly you will be raised up on the Day of Resurrection. (23:17) Certainly We have created above you seven tiers. We have not been ones who are heedless of the creation. (23:18) We sent forth water from heaven in measure and We lodged it in the earth; and We are ones who have the power to take away. (23:19) And We caused to grow for you gardens of date palm trees and grapevines where there is much sweet fruit for you and you eat of it (23:20) and a tree that goes

forth from the mountain of Sinai that bears oil and it is a seasoning for the ones who eat it. (23:21) And truly for you in the flocks there is a lesson; We satiate you with what is in their bellies. In them are many uses (23:22) and of them you eat and on them and on boats you were to be carried.

(23:78) And He it is Who has caused you to grow, have the ability to hear and sight and mind. But little you are thankful! (23:79) It is He Who has made you numerous on the earth and to Him you will be assembled. (23:80) And it is He Who gives life and causes to die and His is the alteration of nighttime and daytime. Will you not then be reasonable? (23:81) Nay! They said the like of what the ancient ones had said: (23:82) They said: When we are dead and have become earth dust and bones, will we certainly be ones who were to be raised up? (23:83) Certainly we were to be promised this—we and our fathers—before this. This is nothing but the fables of the ancient ones. (23:84) Say: To whom belongs the earth and whoever is in it if you had been knowing? (23:85) They will say: To God! Say: Will you then not recollect? (23:86) Say: Who is the Lord of the seven heavens and Lord of the Sublime Throne? (23:87) They will say: It belongs to God! Say: Then will you not be Godfearing? (23:88) Say: In whose hand is the kingship of everything and He grants protection? No one is to be grant protection against Him if you had been knowing. (23:89) They will say: It belongs to God! Say: How then are you under a spell! (23:90) Nay! We have brought them The Truth and truly they are ones who lie. (23:91) God has not taken to Himself a son nor has there been any god along with Him. For then each god would have taken away what he had created. And some of them would have ascended over others. Glory be to God above all that they allege! (23:92) He is the One Who Has Knowledge of the unseen and the visible. Exalted be He over the partners they make with Him.

(23:115) Assumed you that We created you in amusement and that to Us you would not be returned? (23:116) So exalted be God! The true King; there is no god but He, the Lord of the Generous Throne! (23:117) And whoever calls with God another god of which he has no proof, then truly his reckoning is with his Lord. Truly the ones who are ungrateful will not prosper. (23:118) And say: My Lord! Forgive and have mercy and Thou art the Best of the ones who are the most merciful.

Chapter 24 The Light 9 Signs

(24:35) God is the Light of the heavens and the earth. The parable of His Light is as a niche in which there is a lamp; the lamp is in a glass; the glass is as if it had been a glittering star, to be lit from the oil of a blessed olive tree, neither eastern nor western, whose oil is about to illuminate although no fire touches it. Light on light, God guides to His Light whom He wills! And God propounds parables for humanity, and God is Knowing of everything. (24:36) The Light is lit in houses God gave permission to be lifted up and that His Name be remembered in it. Glorify Him in the first part of the day and the eventide (24:37) by men whom neither trade nor trading diverts from the remembrance of God and performing the formal prayer and the giving of purifying alms for they fear a Day when the hearts will go to and fro and their sight,

(24:41) Hast thou not considered that God is glorified by whoever is in the heavens and the earth and the birds, ones spreading their wings; each knows its prayer and its glorification, and God is Knowing of what they accomplish. (24:42) And to God belongs the dominion of the heavens and the earth; and to God is the Homecoming. (24:43) Hast thou not considered how God propels clouds and after that brings them together. After that He lays them into a heap. Thou seest the rain drops go forth in the midst. And He sends down from the heaven mountains of rain in which there is hail. And He lights it on whom He wills and turns away from it whom He wills; the gleams of His lightning almost take away the sight. (24:44) God turns round and round the nighttime and the daytime. Truly in this is a lesson for those who have insight. (24:45) God created every moving creature from water; among them there is what walks on its belly and of them there is what walks on two feet and of them there is what walks on four. God creates what He wills. Truly God is Powerful over everything.

(24:64) Surely to God belongs whatever is in the heavens and the earth. Surely He knows what your hands have done. And on the Day when they are returned to Him, then He will tell them what their hands have done, and God is Knowing of everything.

Chapter 25 The Criterion 14 Signs

(25:1) Blessed was He Who sent down the Criterion between right and wrong to His servant so that perhaps he may be a warner to the worlds, (25:2) He to Whom belongs the dominion of the heavens and the earth, and Who took not to Himself a son. And there is no associate for Him in the dominion and He created everything and has ordained it a foreordaining.

(25:45) Hast thou not considered how thy Lord stretched out the shade. And had He willed, He would have made it still. After that We made the sun an indicator over it. (25:46) Then We seized it to Us an easy seizing. (25:47) And it is He Who makes the nighttime a garment for you and sleep a rest and makes the daytime for a rising. (25:48) And it is He Who sends the winds as that which bears the good tidings before His Mercy. And We sent forth undefiled water from heaven (25:49) that We may give life by it to a lifeless land and with it We satiate. We have created flocks on it and many men.

(25:53) And it is He Who has let forth the two seas— this, agreeable and water of the sweetest kind and this, salty, bitter. Between the two is that which was unapproachable, banned barrier. (25:54) And it is He Who created a mortal from water and has made blood kindred for him and kin by marriage, and thy Lord has been ever Powerful.

(25:58) And put your trust in the Living Who is Undying and glorify His praise. And He has sufficed to be aware of the impieties of His servants (25:59) Who created the heavens and the earth and all that is between the two in six days. After that He turned His attention to the Throne. The Merciful: Ask the aware then about Him. (25:60) And when it was said to them: Prostrate yourselves to The Merciful, they said: And what is The Merciful? Will we prostrate ourselves to what thou hast commanded us? And it increased aversion in them. (25:61) Blessed is He Who made constellations in the heaven and has made in it a light-giving lamp and an illuminating moon. (25:62) And He it is Who made the nighttime and the daytime to follow in succession for whom He had wanted to recollect or He had wanted thankfulness.

Chapter 26 The Poets 12 Signs

(26:78) Who has created me. (26:79) And it is He Who guides me. And it is He, He Who feeds me and gives me drink. (26:80) And when I am sick, it is He Who heals me (26:81) and Who causes me to die, then will give me life, (26:82) and from Whom I am desirous that He will forgive me my transgressions on the Day of Judgment. (26:83) My Lord! Bestow on me critical judgment, and cause me to join with the ones who are in accord with morality. (26:84) And assign me a good repute in the later generations (26:85) and make me one who is an inheritor of the Garden of Bliss. (26:86) And forgive my father. Truly he had been of the ones who go astray. (26:87) And cover me not with shame on a Day they will be raised up, (26:88) on a Day neither wealth will profit nor children (26:89) but him who approaches God with a pure-hearted heart.

Chapter 27 The Ant 13 Signs

(27:25) So they prostrate themselves not to God Who brings out what is hidden in the heavens and the earth and knows what you conceal and what you speak openly. (27:26) God, there is no god but He, the Lord of the Sublime Throne.

(27:60) Is not He better Who created the heavens and the earth and sent forth for you from the heavens water; with it We cause joyous, fertile gardens to develop? It has not been for you to cause their trees to develop, is there any god besides God? Nay! They are a folk who equate others with God! (27:61) Is not He better Who made the earth a stopping place and made rivers in its midst and made firm mountains for it and made between the two seas that which hinders, is there a god besides God? Nay! But most of them know not! (27:62) Is not He better Who answers one who was constrained when he calls to Him and He removes the evil and assigns you as viceregents on the earth, is there a god besides God? Little is what you recollect! Is not He better Who guides you in the shadows of the dry land and the sea and Who sends the winds, that which bears good tidings before His mercy, is there a god besides God? Exalted is God above all the partners that they make with Him! (27:63) Is not He better Who begins creation, after that will cause it to return and Who provides you from the heavens and the earth, is there a god besides God? (27:64) Say: Bring forth your proof if you have been ones who are sincere! (27:65) Say: None knows who is in the heavens and the earth nor the unseen but God. Nor are they aware when they will be raised up.

(27:73) And truly thy Lord is Possessor of Grace for humanity, but most of them thank Him not. (27:74) And truly thy Lord knows what their breasts hide and what they speak openly. (27:75) There is nothing of the unseen in the heaven and the earth, but that it is in the clear Book.

(27:78) Truly thy Lord will decree between them with His determination. And He is The Almighty, The Knowing. (27:79) So put thy trust in God; truly thou art on The clear Truth.

Chapter 28 The Story 7 Signs

(28:68) And thy Lord creates whatever He wills and chooses, there had not been a choice for them. Glory be to God and exalted is He above all the partners they make with Him! (28:69) And thy Lord knows what their breasts hide and what they speak openly. (28:70) And He, God, there is no god but He; His is all Praise in the First and in the Last; and His is the determination and to Him you will be returned. (28:71) Say: Have you yourself considered what if God had made the night endless for you until the Day of Resurrection? What god other than God brings you illumination? Will you not then hear? (28:72) Say: Have you yourselves considered what if God had made the daytime endless for you until the Day of Resurrection? What god other than God brings you nighttime wherein you may rest? Will you not then perceive? (28:73) And it is out of His mercy that He has assigned for you the nighttime and the daytime that you may rest in it and that you may be looking for His grace and so that perhaps you will be thankful.

(28:88) And call not to any god other than God. There is no god but He! Everything is perishing but His Countenance. To Him is the determination and to Him you will be returned.

Chapter 29 The Spider 9 Signs

(29:19) Have they not considered how God causes the

creation to begin then He causes it to return? Truly that for God is easy. (29:20) Say: Move throughout the earth and look on how He began the creation. After that God will cause the last growth to grow. Truly God is Powerful over everything. (29:21) He punishes whom He wills and has mercy on whom He wills; and to Him you will come back. (29:22) You will not be ones who frustrate Him on the earth nor in the heaven; and there is not for you other than God either a protector nor a helper.

(29:60) And so many a moving creature carries not its own provision, but God provides for it and for you. And He is The Hearing, The Knowing. (29:61) And if you were to ask them: Who created the heavens and the earth and caused the sun and the moon to be subservient? They will certainly say: God; how then are they mislead! (29:62) God extends the provision for whom He will of His servants and confines it for whom He will. Truly God is Knowing of everything. (29:63) And if thou wert to ask them: Who sends down water from heaven and gives life by it to the earth after its death, certainly they would say: God! Say: The Praise belongs to God! Nay! Most of them are not reasonable. (29:64) And this present life is not but a diversion and a pastime. And truly the Last Abode is the eternal life, if they had been knowing!

Chapter 30 The Romans 17 Signs

(30:17) So glory be to God at the time of the evening hour and at the time when it comes to be in the morning! (30:18) To Him be The Praise in the heavens and the earth and in the evening and at the time of noon. (30:19) He brings out the living from the dead and He brings out the dead from the living and He gives life to the earth after death. And thus you will be brought out. (30:20) And among His signs are that He created you from earth dust. After that, lo and behold! You were mortals diffused. (30:21) And among His signs are that He created for you wives from among your-selves, that you may rest in them and He has made affection and mercy among you. Truly in that are certainly signs for a folk who reflect. (30:22) And among His signs are the cre-ation of the heavens and the earth and the alteration of your languages and hues. Truly in that are certainly signs for all beings who have knowledge. (30:23) And among His signs are your slumbering by nighttime and by daytime and your looking for His grace. Truly in that are certainly signs for a folk who hear. (30:24) And among His signs are that He causes you to see the lightning in fear and in hope and He sends water down from heaven and gives life by it to the earth after its death. Truly in that are certainly signs for a folk who are reasonable. (30:25) And among His signs are that the heaven and the earth are secured for you by His command. When He will call you by a call after that from the earth, lo and behold! You will go forth! (30:26) And to Him belongs whoever is in the heavens and the earth. All are ones who are morally obligated to Him. (30:27) And He it is Who begins the creation. After that He causes it to return and this is insignificant for Him. And His is the Lofty Parable in the heavens and the earth. And He is The Almighty, The Wise.

(30:40) God is He Who created you. After that He pro-vided for you and after that He will cause you to die. After that He will give you life; has anyone of the partners you have made with Him accomplished anything of that? Glory be to Him! Exalted is He above what that they associate with Him!

(30:46) Among His signs are that He sends the winds as ones that give good tidings and causes you to experience His mercy and so that the boats may run at His command and that you be looking for His grace so that perhaps you would be thankful.

(30:48) God is He Who sends the winds so they stir up clouds. He extends them in the heaven how He wills and He makes them into pieces until you see rain drops go forth from their midst; then when He has made them light on whomever He wills of His servants, lo and behold! They rejoice at the good tidings. (30:49) And truly they have been —even before it is sent down on them— ones who are seized with despair. (30:50) Look on the effects of the mercy of God, how He is One Who Gives Life to the earth after its death! Truly that! He is One Who Gives Life to the dead and He is Powerful over everything.

(30:54) God is He Who created you in your weakness. After that weakness He assigned strength; then after that strength He assigned weakness and grey hair. And He creates what He wills; and He is The Knowing, The Powerful.

Chapter 31 Luqman 8 Signs

(31:10) He has created the heavens without any pillars so that you see the heavens. And He has cast firm mountains on the earth so that the earth should not vibrate with you and He disseminated in and on it of every moving creature. And We sent forth water from heaven and We caused every generous kind to develop in it.

(31:20) Have you not considered that God has caused to become subservient to you whatever is in the heavens and whatever is in and on the earth and has lavished on you His divine blessing, that which is manifest and that which is inward, and yet of humanity is he who disputes about God without knowledge and without guidance and without an illuminating Book.

(31:26) To God belongs whatever is in the heavens and the earth. Truly God, He is The Sufficient, The Worthy of Praise. (31:27) And if trees on the earth were only pens and the sea was caused to increase after that with seven more seas that were ink, yet the Words of God would not come to an end, truly God is Almighty, Wise. (31:28) Your creation and your Uprising are not but like that of a single soul, truly God is Hearing, Seeing. (31:29) Hast thou not considered that God causes the nighttime to be inserted into the daytime and causes the daytime to be inserted into the nighttime and causes the sun to become subservient and the moon, each running for a term, that which was determined and that God is Aware of that you do? (31:30) That is because God, He is The Truth, and what they call to other than Him is falsehood. And that God, He is The Lofty, The Great! (31:31) Hast thou not considered that the boats run through the sea by the divine blessing of God that He may cause you to see His signs? Truly in that are signs for every enduring, grateful one.

Chapter 32 The Prostration 7 Signs

(32:4) God! It is He Who created the heavens and the earth and all that is between them in six days. After that He turned His attention to the Throne; you have none other than Him as protector and no intercessor. Will you not then recollect? (32:5) He manages every command from the heaven to the earth. After that it will go up to Him in a day, the span of which has been a thousand years of what you number. (32:6) That is the One Who has Knowledge of the unseen and the visible, The Almighty, The Compassionate (32:7) Who did everything that He created well; and He began the creation of the human being from clay. (32:8) After that He made mankind's progeny from the extraction of despicable water. (32:9) After that He shaped him and breathed into him His Sprit. And He made for you the ability to hear and sight and minds. But you give little thanks!

(32:27) Have they not considered that We drive water to the barren dust of earth? We drive out crops with it from which their flocks eat and they themselves; will they not then perceive?

Chapter 34 Sheba 5 Signs

(34:1) The Praise belongs to God; to Him belongs whatever is in the heavens and whatever is in and on the earth and His is The Praise in the world to come. And He is The Wise, The Aware. (34:2) He knows whatever penetrates into the earth and what goes forth out of it and what goes forth from the heaven and what comes down from it. And He is The Compassionate, The Forgiving. (34:3) And those who disbelieve said: The Hour will not approach us; say: Yea! By my Lord it will certainly approach you. He is One Who has Knowledge of the Unseen; not an atom's weight escapes from Him in the heavens or in and on the earth, be it smaller than that or greater, but that it has been in a clear Book

(34:9) Have they not considered what is in advance of them and what is behind them of the heaven and the earth? If We will, We could cause the earth to swallow them or drop on them pieces of heaven. Truly in this is certainly a sign for every repentant servant.

(34:36) Say: Truly my Lord extends the provision for whom He wills and confines it for whom He wills except most of humanity knows not.

Chapter 35 The Originator 13 Signs

(35:1) The Praise belongs to God, One Who is the Originator of the heavens and the earth, the One Who Makes the angels messengers with wings by twos and threes and fours. He increases in creation what He wills. Truly God is Powerful over everything. (35:2) Whatever God may open of mercy to humanity, there is not one who holds it back; and what He holds back, there is not one who sends it after that. And He is The Almighty, The Wise. (35:3) O humanity! Remember the divine blessing of God on you! Is there any creator other than God Who provides for you from heaven and the earth? There is no god but He; how then are you misled!

(35:9) And it is God Who sent the winds so that they stir up the clouds and We drive them to a dead land and We give life by them to the earth after its death. Thus will be the rising! (35:10) Whoever has been wanting great glory, great glory belongs to God altogether. To Him Words of what is good rise and He exalts an act in accord with morality. But those who plan evil deeds, for them will be a severe punishment; and the planning of those will come to nothing. (35:11) After that God created you from earth dust, and after that from seminal fluid and He made you pairs after that. And no female carries nor brings forth a baby but with His Knowledge. And no one is given a long life nor is anything reduced from his lifetime but it is in a Book. Truly that is easy for God. (35:12) The two bodies of water are not on the same level. This is agreeable, water of the sweetest kind and delicious to drink and the other is salty and bitter; but from both you eat succulent flesh and pull out glitter that you wear; and you see the boats, that which plows through the waves on it, that you may be looking for His grace and so that perhaps you would be thankful. (35:13) He causes the nighttime to be inserted in the daytime and He causes the daytime to be inserted into the nighttime and He causes the sun to become subservient and the moon. Each runs its course for a term, that was determined. That is God, your Lord. For Him is the dominion! And those whom you call other than Him possess not even the skin of a date stone.

(35:27) Hast thou not considered that God sent forth water from the heavens? And then We brought out fruits, ones of varying hues. Among the mountains are white and red streaks —ones of varying hues— and others raven black, (35:28) and of humanity and moving creatures and flocks, thus they are likewise hues, ones that are at variance, only those of His servants who dread God are knowing, truly God is Almighty, Forgiving.

(35:41) Truly God holds back the heavens and the earth so that they are not displaced. And if they are displaced, there is none who holds them back but He. Truly He has been Forbearing, Forgiving.

(35:44) And have they not journeyed on the earth and looked on how had been the Ultimate End of those who were before them and they had been stronger than they are in strength? And God has not been weakened by anything in the heavens nor in or on the earth. Truly He has been Knowing, Powerful. (35:45) And if God were to take humanity to task for what they have earned, He would not leave on the back of the earth any moving creature, but He postpones to a term that was determined; and when their term has drawn near, then truly God has been Seeing of His servants.

Chapter 36 Ya Sin 25 Signs

(36:33) And a sign for them is the dead body of the earth. We gave life to it and We brought out grain from it so that they ate from it. (36:34) We have made in them gardens of date palm trees and grapevines and We have caused a spring to gush forth in it (36:35) so that they may eat of the fruits from there that their hands have not made; will they then not be thankful? (36:36) Glory be to Him Who created pairs, all of them, of what the earth causes to develop as well as of their own kind and of what they know not! (36:37) And a sign for them is the nighttime. We pluck the daytime from it and lo and behold! They are in darkness! (36:38) And the sun runs to a resting place for it. That is foreordained by The Almighty, The Knowing. (36:39) And for the moon We have ordained mansions until it reverts like an ripe aged, dry, date stalk. (36:40) It is not fit and proper for the sun to overtake the moon nor the nighttime to outstrip the daytime. They each swim in an orbit. (36:41) A sign for them is that We carried their offspring in a laden boat. (36:42) And We have created for them of its like that they ride. (36:43) And if We will, We will drown them. There will be none who cries aloud for help for them nor will they be saved (36:44) unless it be a mercy from Us and as an enjoyment for a while.

(36:71) Have they not considered how We have created for them out of what Our hands have done flocks, so have they become of them ones who are possessors? (36:72) And We have subdued them for them so that of them, some are riding animals and some of them, they eat. (36:73) And they have uses from them and a drinking place; will they not then be thankful? (36:74) And they have taken to themselves gods other than God so that perhaps they would be helped. (36:75) They are not able to help them while they are to them as a charged army. (36:76) So let not their saying grieve you. Truly We know what they keep secret and what they speak openly. (36:77) Has the human being not considered that We have created him from seminal fluid? Then lo and behold! He becomes a clear adversary. (36:78) He propounds parables for Us and forgets his own creation. He said: Who will give life to these bones when they have decayed? (36:79) Say: He will give life to them Who caused them to grow the first time and He is The Knowing of every creation. (36:80) It is He Who makes for you fire out of a green tree. Lo and behold! You kindle from it. (36:81) Is not He Who created the heavens and the earth One Who has the Power to create the like of them? Yea! And He is The Knowing Creator. (36:82) Truly His command when He wants a thing is but to say to it: Be! (36:83) Then it is! Then Glory be to Him in whose hand is the Kingship of everything! And to Him you will be returned.

Chapter 37 The Ones Standing in Ranks 14 Signs

(37:1) By the ones standing in ranks, ranged in rows

(37:2) then those who scare in a scaring (37:3) then ones who recount the Remembrance, (37:4) truly your God is certainly One, (37:5) the Lord of the heavens and the earth and all that is between them and the Lord of the sunrise. (37:6) Truly We have made to appear pleasing the present heaven with the adornment of the stars (37:7) and kept safe from every emboldened Satan. (37:8) They pay no attention to the lofty Council for they are hurled at from every edge, (37:9) rejected; and for them is a punishment, that which lasts forever, (37:10) but for him who snatches a fragment, then a piercing flame pursues him. (37:11) So ask them for advice: Are they stronger in constitution or those others whom We have created? Truly We have created them of clinging clay.

(37:180) Glory be to thy Lord, the Lord of Great Glory, from what they allege about Him. (37:181) And peace be to the ones who were sent. (37:182) And The Praise belongs to God, the Lord of the worlds!

Chapter 38 Sad 4 Signs

(38:65) Say: I am only one who warns; and there is no god but God, The One, The Omniscient, (38:66) the Lord of the heavens and the earth and all that is between them, The Almighty, The Forgiver. (38:67) Say: It is a serious tiding (38:68) from which you are ones who turn aside.

Chapter 39 The Troops 16 Signs

(39:4) Had God wanted to take to Himself a son, He would have favored from what He had created of what He wills. Glory be to Him; He is God, The One, The Omniscient. (39:5) He has created the heavens and the earth with The Truth; He wraps up the nighttime around the daytime and wraps up the daytime around the nighttime; and He has caused to become subservient the sun and the moon; each running for a term, that which was determined, is He not

The Almighty, The Forgiving? (39:6) He created you from one soul. After that He made its mate from it and He has sent forth for you eight pairs of flocks. He creates you in the wombs of your mothers, creation after creation, in threefold shadows. Such is God your Lord. His is the dominion; there is no god but He; why then are you turned away?

(39:21) Hast thou not considered that God has sent forth water from heaven and threads fountains in the earth, then brings out crops by it of hues, ones that are at variance. After that they wither so thou seest them as ones that were growing yellow. Then He makes them chaff. Truly in this is a reminder for those who have intuition. (39:22) Is he whose breast God has expanded for submission, is he in a light from His Lord? So woe to those whose hearts are hardened against the Remembrance of God. They are clearly going astray.

(39:36) Is not God One Who Suffices for His servants; they frighten thee with those besides Him. And whom God causes to go astray, there is not for him any one who guides. (39:37) And whomever God guides, there is not for him anyone who leads astray, is not God Almighty, The Possessor of Requital? (39:38) And truly if you ask them: Who created the heavens and the earth? They would certainly say: God. Say: Have you yourselves considered the things that you call to other than God? If God wants some distress for me, would they be ones who remove His distress from me? Or if He wants some mercy for me would they (f) be ones who hold back His mercy? Say: God is enough for me; in Him put their trust the ones who put their trust.

(39:42) God calls the souls to Himself at the time of their death and those that have not died during their slumbering; He holds back those for whom He has decreed death and sends the others back for a term, that which was determined. Truly in that are signs for a folk who reflect.

(39:46) Say: O God! One Who is Originator of the heavens and the earth! One Who Has Knowledge of the unseen and the visible! Thou shalt give judgment among Thy servants about what they had been at variance in it.

(39:67) And they measure not God with His true measure and the earth altogether will be His handful. On the Day of Resurrection the heavens will be rolled up in His right hand. Glory be to Him! And exalted is He above all the partners they make with Him! (39:68) And the trumpet will be blown. Then whoever is in the heavens will swoon and whoever is in and on the earth, but he whom God willed; after that it will be blown another time. Then they will be upright looking on. (39:69) And the earth will shine with the Light of its Lord and the Book will be laid down and the prophets and the witnesses will be brought. And it will be decided among them with The Truth. And they will not be done wrong. (39:70) The account of each soul would shall be paid in full for what it has done. He is greater in knowledge of what they accomplish.

(39:74) They would say: The Praise belongs to God Who has been sincere in His promise to us and has given us the earth as inheritance that we may take our dwelling in the Garden wherever we will; how excellent a compensation for ones who work! (39:75) And thou wilt see the angels as ones who encircle around the Throne glorifying their Lord with praise; and it would be decided in Truth among them and it would be said: The Praise belongs to God, the Lord of the worlds.

Chapter 40 The One Who Forgives 19 Signs

(40:1) Ḥā Mīm. (40:2) The sending down successively of this Book is from God, The Almighty, The Knower, (40:3) The One Who Forgives impieties and The One Who Accepts remorse, The Severe in Repayment, The Possessor of Bounty;

there is no god but He; to Him is the Homecoming.

(40:7) Those who carry the Throne and all those around it who glorify the praises of their Lord and believe in Him and ask forgiveness for those who have believed say: Our Lord! Thou hast encompassed everything in mercy and in knowledge. So forgive those who have repented and have followed Thy way and guard them from the punishment of hellfire.

(40:13) It is He Who causes you to see His signs and sends down provision for you from heaven. And none recollect but those who are penitent. (40:14) So call you on God ones who are sincere and devoted. in the way of life to Him although the ones who are ungrateful may dislike it. (40:15) Exalter of Degrees, Possessor of the Throne, He casts the Spirit by His command on whom He wills of His servants that He may warn of the Day of Encounter, (40:16) a Day when they are ones who depart; nothing about them will be hidden from God. Whose is the dominion this Day; it is to God, The One, The Omniscient. (40:17) On this Day every soul will be given recompense for what it has earned. There will be no injustice today. God is Swift in reckoning.

(40:61) God is He Who has made for you the nighttime so that you may rest in it and the daytime for one who perceives. Truly God is full of grace to humanity, except most of humanity is not thankful. (40:62) That is God, your Lord, the Creator of all things. There is no god but He; how then are you misled? (40:63) Thus are misled those who have been negating the signs of God. (40:64) God is He Who has made the earth for you as a stopping place and the heaven as a canopy. And He has formed you and formed you well and He has provided you of what is good. That is God, your Lord; then blessed be God, the Lord of the worlds! (40:65) He is The Living! There is no god but He! So call to Him ones sincere and devoted in the way of life to Him, the Praise belongs to God, the Lord of the worlds!

(40:67) He it is Who created you from earth dust, after that from seminal fluid and after that from a clot. Then He brings you out as infant children. After that you come of age and are fully grown and after that you are an old man. And of you is he whom death calls to itself before; and that you reach a term, that which was determined so that perhaps you would be reasonable. (40:68) He it is Who gives life and causes to die; and when He decrees an affair, He not but says to it: Be! Then it is!

(40:79) God is He Who has made for you flocks that you may ride on some of them and eat some of them. (40:80) And you have what is profitable from them and that with them you may reach the satisfaction of a need that is in your breasts and may be carried on them as on boats. (40:81) And He causes you to see His signs . So which of the signs of God do you reject?

Chapter 41 They Were Explained Distinctly 12 Signs

(41:9) Say: Truly were you ungrateful to Him Who created the earth in two days? And assigned you to Him rivals? That is the Lord of the worlds! (41:10) And He made on it firm mountains from above it and He blessed it and ordained its sustenance within it in four days equal for ones who seek. (41:11) After that He turned His attention to the heaven while it was smoke and He said to it and to the earth: Approach both of you willing or unwilling. They both said: We approach as ones who are obedient. (41:12) Then He foreordained seven heavens in two days and He revealed in each heaven its command. We made the present heaven appear pleasing with lamps and keeping them safe. Such is the decree of the Almighty, The Knowing.

(41:37) And of His signs are the nighttime and the daytime and the sun and the moon. Prostrate not to the sun nor to the moon, but prostrate to God Who created the two of them if it is He you worship. (41:38) But if they grow arrogant, then those who are with thy Lord glorify Him during the nighttime and daytime and they never grow weary.‡ (41:39) And among His signs are that you see the earth as that which is humble; but when We send forth water to it, it quivers and swells.

(41:45) And certainly We gave Moses the Book, then there was variance in it, and had it not been for a Word that had preceded from thy Lord, it was to be decided between them. But truly they are in uncertainty, ones whose suspicions have been aroused. (41:46) Whoever has acted in accord with morality, it is for himself; and whoever does evil, it is against himself, and thy Lord is not unjust to His servants. (41:47) To Him is returned the knowledge of the Hour. No fruits go forth from their sheaths and no female conceives or brings forth offspring but with His knowledge. And on a Day He will cry out to them: Where are My associates? They would say: We proclaim to Thee that none of us was a witness to that.

(41:53) We will cause them to see Our signs on the horizons and within their own selves until it becomes clear to them that it is The Truth, suffices not thy Lord that truly He is Witness over all things? (41:54) They are in hesitancy about the meeting with their Lord, truly He is who One Who Encloses everything.

Chapter 42 The Consultation 16 Signs

(42:1) Ḥā Mīm. (42:2) ʿAyn Sīn Qāf. (42:3) Thus He reveals to thee and to those who were before thee, God is The Almighty, The Wise. (42:4) To Him belongs whatever is in the heavens and whatever is in the earth; and He is The Lofty, The Sublime. (42:5) The heavens were about to split asunder from above them. And when the angels glorify the praise of their Lord and ask forgiveness for those on the earth; truly God, He is The Forgiving, The Compassionate.

(42:11) One Who is Originator of the heavens and the earth. He has made for you mates of yourselves and of the flocks, mates; by which means He makes you numerous in it. There is not like Him anything; and He is The Hearing, The Seeing. (42:12) To Him belong the keys of the heavens and the earth; He extends provision for whomever He will and measures it. Truly He is The Knowing of everything.

(42:28) And He it is Who sends down plenteous rain water after they have despaired and He unfolds His mercy. And He is The Protector, The Worthy of Praise. (42:29) And among His signs are the creation of the heavens and the earth and whatever of moving creatures He has disseminated in them. And He has the power of amassing them when He wills.

(42:32) And among His signs are the ones that run on the sea like landmarks. (42:33) If He wills, He may still the wind. Then they would stay motionless on the surface. Truly in that are signs for every enduring and grateful one.

(42:49) To God belongs the dominion of the heavens and the earth. He creates what He wills. He bestows females on whom He wills and bestows males on whom He wills (42:50) or He couples them, males and females; and He makes barren whom He wills. Truly He is Knowing, Powerful. (42:51) And it had not been for a mortal that God should speak to him, but by revelation or from behind a partition or that He send a Messenger to reveal by His permission what He wills. Truly He is Lofty, Wise. (42:52) And thus We have revealed to thee the Spirit of Our command. Thou wert not informed what the Book is nor what is belief, but We have made it a light by which We guide whomever We will of Our servants. And truly thou, thou guidest to a straight path— (42:53) the path of God, to whom belongs whatever is in the heavens and whatever is in and on the earth, truly to God all affairs come home.

Chapter 43 The Ornaments 16 Signs

(43:9) And certainly if you ask them: Who has created the heavens and the earth? They will certainly say: The Almighty, The Knowing created them, (43:10) Who has made the earth a cradle for you and has made in it ways for you so that perhaps you would be truly guided (43:11) and Who sends down water from heaven in measure. Then We revive with it a lifeless land. Thus you are brought out. (43:12) And it is He Who created all the pairs and has assigned for you the boats and the flocks on which you ride (43:13) so that you may sit upon their backs and after that you may remember the divine blessing of your Lord when you are seated on them and you say: Glory be to Him Who causes this to become subservient to us and we have not been ones who are equal to it! (43:14) And truly we certainly are to our Lord ones who are turning.

(43:80) Assume they that We hear not their secret thoughts and their conspiring secretly? Yea! Our messengers are near them writing down. (43:81) Say: If The Merciful had a son, then I would be the first of ones who worship. (43:82) Glory be to the Lord of the heavens and the earth, the Lord of the Throne, from all that they allege! (43:83) So let them engage in idle talk and to play until they encounter their Day which they are promised. (43:84) And it is He Who is in the heaven, God, and on the earth, God. And He is The Wise, The Knowing. (43:85) Blessed is He to whom belongs the dominion of the heavens and the earth and whatever is between them and with Whom is the knowledge of the Hour and to Whom will you be returned. (43:86) And those whom they call to possess no power other than Him for intercession, only those who bear witness to The Truth, and they know. (43:87) And if you ask them: Who created them? They will certainly say: God; how then are they misled? (43:88) And his saying: O my Lord! Truly these are a folk who believe not (43:89) so overlook them and say: Peace. And soon they will know.

Chapter 44 The Smoke 4 Signs

(44:7) Lord of the heavens and the earth and whatever is between them; if you had been ones who are certain. (44:8) There is no god but He. It is He Who gives life and causes to die; He is your Lord and the Lord of your ancient fathers.

(44:38) And We created not the heavens and the earth and all that is between them as ones who play! (44:39) We created them not but with The Truth except most of them know not.

Chapter 45 The Ones Who Kneel 9 Signs

(45:1) Ḥā Mīm. (45:2) The sending down the Book successively is from God, The Almighty, The Wise. (45:3) Truly in the heavens and the earth are signs for the ones who believe. (45:4) And in your creation and what He disseminated of moving creatures are signs for a folk who are certain, (45:5) the alternation of the nighttime and the daytime and what God has sent forth from the heaven of provision. He gives life with it to the earth after its death and the diversifying of the winds— signs for a folk who are reasonable.

(45:12) God it is He Who has caused the sea to become subservient to you that the boats may run through it by His command and so that you may look for His grace and perhaps you will be thankful. (45:13) And He has caused to become subservient for you whatever is in the heavens and whatever is in and on the earth. All is from Him. Truly in that are signs for a folk who reflect.

(45:36) So The Praise belongs to God, the Lord of the

heavens and the Lord of the earth, and the Lord of the worlds. (45:37) And His is the dominion of the heavens and the earth; and He is The Almighty, The Wise.

Chapter 46 The Curving Sandhills 4 Signs

(46:1) Ḥā Mīm. (46:2) The sending down successively of the Book is from God The Almighty, The Wise. (46:3) We have not created the heavens and the earth and whatever is between the two but with The Truth and for a term, that which was determined. And those who are ungrateful from what they were to be warned about are ones who turn aside.

(46:33) Have they not considered that God Who created the heavens and the earth and was not wearied by their creation— is One Who Has Power to give life to the dead. Yea! He truly is Powerful over all things.

Chapter 48 The Victory 1 Sign

(48:14) And to God belongs the dominion of the heavens and the earth. He forgives whom He wills and punishes whom He wills. And God has been Forgiving, Compassionate.

Chapter 50 Qaf 7 Signs

(50:6) Looked they not on the heaven above them, how We have built it and made it appear pleasing? And there are not any gaps in it. (50:7) And the earth, We have stretched it out and cast on it firm mountains and have caused to develop in it of every diverse pair (50:8) for contemplation and as a reminder to every repentant servant. (50:9) And We sent down blessed water from heaven. Then We caused gardens to develop from it and reaped grains of wheat (50:10) and high-reaching date palm trees with ranged spathes (50:11) as provision for My servants; and We gave life by them to a lifeless land. Thus will be the going forth.

(50:16) And certainly We have created the human being. We know what evil his soul whispers to him; We are nearer to him than the jugular vein.

Chapter 51 The Winnowing Winds 7 Signs

(51:20) On the earth are signs for the ones who are certain (51:21 and in yourselves. Will you not then perceive? (51:22) And in the heaven is your provision as you are promised (51:23) by the Lord of the heaven and the earth. It is truly The Truth just as you yourself speak.

(51:47) And We built the heaven with potency and truly We are ones who extend wide. (51:48) And the earth, We have spread it forth. How excellent are the ones who spread! (51:49) And of everything We have created mates so that perhaps you would recollect.

Chapter 53 The Star 8 Signs

(53:42) And that towards thy Lord is the Utmost Boundary. (53:43) And that it is He, He Who causes laughter and causes weeping. (53:44) And it is He, He Who causes to die and gives life (53:45) and that it is He, He created the pairs, male and female, (53:46) from seminal fluid when it is emitted; (53:47) and that with Him is another growth; (53:48) and that it is He, He Who Enriched and made rich; (53:49) and that it is He, He Who is the Lord of Sirius;

Chapter 54 The Moon 7 Signs

(54:49) Truly We have created all things in measure (54:50) and Our command is not but one as the twinkling of the eye. (54:51) And certainly We have caused to perish their partisans. Is there then one who recalls? (54:52) And each and everything they have accomplished is in the ancient scrolls. (54:53) And every small and great thing is that which was inscribed. (54:54) Truly the ones who are Godfearing will be in Gardens and rivers, (54:55) in a position of sincerity near an Omnipotent King.

Chapter 55 The Merciful 27 Signs

(55:1) The Merciful. (55:2) He taught the Quran. (55:3) He created the human being. (55:4) He taught him the clear explanation. (55:5) The sun and the moon are to keep count. (55:6) And the stars and the trees both prostrate. (55:7) And the heaven He has exalted. And He has set in place the Balance: (55:8) That you be not defiant in the Balance. (55:9) Set up the weight with equity and skimp not in the Balance. (55:10) And He has set the earth in place for the human race. (55:11) On and in it are many kinds of sweet fruit and date palm trees with the sheaths of a fruit tree (55:12) and grain with husks and fragrant herbs. (55:13) So which of the benefits of the Lord of you both will you both deny? (55:14) He created the human being from dry clay like potter's clay. (55:15) He created the spirits from a smokeless flame of fire. (55:16) So which of the benefits of the Lord of you both will you both deny? (55:17) The Lord of the Two Easts, and the Lord of the Two Wests! (55:18) So which of the benefits of the Lord of you both will you both deny? (55:19) He has let forth the two seas to meet each other. (55:20) Between them is a barrier which they wrong not. (55:21) So which of the benefits of the Lord of you both will you both deny? (55:22) From both of them go forth pearls and coral. (55:23) So which of the benefits of the Lord of you both will you both deny? (55:24) His are ones that run with that which was displayed in the sea like landmarks. (55:25) So which of the benefits of the Lord of you both will you both deny? (55:26) All who are in or on it are ones who are being annihilated, (55:27) yet the Countenance of thy Lord will remain forever, Possessor of The Majesty and The Splendor.

Chapter 56 The Inevitable 17 Signs

(56:58) Have you considered what you spill of human seed? (56:59) Is it you who create it or are We the ones who create? (56:60) We have ordained death among you and We are not ones who were to be outstripped (56:61) in that We will substitute your likenesses and cause you to grow in what you know not. (56:62) And surely you have known the first growth. Will you not then recollect? (56:63) Have you considered the soil that you till? (56:64) Is it you who sows it or are We the ones who are sowers? (56:65) If We will, We would make it into chaff and you would continue to joke saying: (56:66) We are ones who are debt-loaded! (56:67) Nay! We are ones who were to be deprived. (56:68) Have you considered the water that you drink? (56:69) Is it you who sends it forth from the cloud vapor or are We the ones who send forth? (56:70) If We will, We would make it bitter. Why then are you not thankful? (56:71) Have you considered the fire which you kindle? (56:72) Is it you who causes the tree to grow or are We the ones who cause it to grow? (56:73) We have made it an admonition and sustenance for ones who are desert people. (56:74) Then glorify with the name of thy Lord, The Sublime.

Chapter 57 Iron 6 Signs

(57:1) Whatever is in the heavens glorifies God and whatever is in and on the earth; and He is The Almighty, The Wise. (57:2) To Him belongs the dominion of the heavens and the earth; He gives life and causes to die; and He is Powerful over all things. (57:3) He is The First and The Last, The One Who is Outward and The One Who is Inward; and He is Knowing of everything. (57:4) It is He Who created the heavens and the earth in six days. Then He turned His attention to the Throne. He knows what penetrates into the earth and what goes forth from it, and what comes down from the heaven and what goes up to it; and He is with you wherever you have been. And God is Seeing of what you do. (57:5) To Him belongs the dominion of the heavens and the earth. All commands return to God. (57:6) He causes the nighttime to be inserted into the daytime and causes the daytime to be inserted into the nighttime. And He is Knowing of whatever is in the breasts.

Chapter 58 She Who Disputes 1 Sign

(58:7) Hast thou not considered that God knows whatever is in the heavens and whatever is in and on the earth; there is no secret conspiring of three, but He is their fourth nor of five, but He is the sixth nor of fewer than that nor of more, but He is with them wherever they might be; after that He will inform them of what they did on the Day of Resurrection. Truly God is Knowing of everything.

Chapter 59 The Banishment 4 Signs

(59:21) If We had sent forth this, the Quran, on a mountain, you would have seen it as one that is humbled, one that is split open from dread of God. And such are the parables that We propound for humanity so that perhaps they would reflect. (59:22) He is God; there is no god but He; The One Who Has Knowledge of the unseen and the visible; He is The Merciful, The Compassionate. (59:23) He is God besides whom there is no god but He, The King, The Holy, The Peaceable, The Bestower, The Preserver The Almighty, The Compeller The One Who is Supreme. Glory be to God, above whatever partners they make with Him. (59:24) He is God, The Creator, The One Who Fashions, The One Who is The Giver of Form; to Him belong the Fairest Names. Whatever is in the heavens glorifies Him and whatever is in and on the earth and He is The Almighty, The Wise.

Chapter 62 The Congregation 4 Signs

(62:1) Whatever is in the heavens glorifies God and whatever is in and on the earth, The King, The Holy, The Almighty, The Wise. (62:2) He it is Who raises up among the unlettered a Messenger from among them recounting His signs to them and making them pure and teaching them the Book and wisdom even though they had been before certainly clearly going astray (62:3) and also to others among them who have not yet joined them. And He is The Almighty, The Wise. (62:4) That is the grace of God. He gives it to whom He wills. And God is Possessor of the Sublime Grace.

Chapter 64 The Mutual Loss and Gain 4 Signs

(64:1) Whatever is in the heavens glorifies God and whatever is in and on the earth; His is the dominion and to Him belongs all the praise; and He is Powerful over everything. (64:2) He it is Who has created you: So some of you are ones who disbelieve and some of you are ones who believe. And God is Seeing of what you do. (64:3) He has created the heavens and the earth with The Truth and He has formed you and formed your forms well; and to Him is the Homecoming! (64:4) He knows what is in the heavens and the earth and He knows what you keep secret and what you speak openly. And God is The Knowing of what is in the breasts.

Chapter 65 Divorce 1 Sign

(65:12) It is God Who created the seven heavens and of the earth, of a similar number like them. The command comes forth between them so that perhaps you would know that God is Powerful over all things and that God truly is One Who Comprehends all things in His Knowledge.

Chapter 67 The Dominion 13 Signs

(67:1) Blessed be He in whose hands is the dominion and He is Powerful over everything! (67:2) He Who has created death and this life that He might try you as to which of you is fairest in action. And He is The Almighty, The Forgiving, (67:3) Who created the seven heavens one on another; thou seest not any imperfection in the creation of The Merciful; then return thy sight! Seest thou any flaw? (67:4) After that return thy sight twice again and thy sight will turn about to thee, one that is dazzled while it is weary. (67:5) And certainly We have made to appear pleasing the lower heaven with lamps and We have assigned them things to stone satans. We have made ready for them the punishment of the blaze.

(67:13) Keep your saying secret or publish it; truly He is Knowing of what is in your breasts. (67:14) Would He who has created not know? And He is The Subtle, The Aware. (67:15) It is He who has made the earth submissive to you, so walk in its tracts and eat of His provision; to Him is the rising.

(67:19) Have they not considered the birds above them ones who are spreading and closing their wings? Nothing holds them back but The Merciful. Truly He is Seeing of everything.

(67:23) Say: It is He who has caused you to grow and assigned you the ability to hear, sight, and minds; yet how little you thank! (67:24) Say: It is He who has made you numerous on the earth and to Him you will be assembled.

(67:29) Say: He is The Merciful. We have believed in Him and in Him we have put our trust; then you will know who is he that is clearly gone astray. (67:30) Say: Have you yourselves considered? If it came to be in the morning that your water be sunk into the ground, then who will come to you with assistance?

Chapter 71 Noah 10 Signs

(71:11) He will cause the heavens to send abundant rain to you. (71:12) He will furnish you relief with wealth and children. And He will assign for you Gardens and will assign for you rivers. (71:13) What is it with you that you hope not for dignity from God (71:14) since He created you in stages? (71:15) Have you not considered how God created the seven heavens, one stage on another? (71:16) And He made the moon in them as a light-giving lamp and made the sun as a burning lamp? (71:17) And God caused you to develop and brought you forth from the earth. (71:18) After that He will cause you to return into it and bring you out in an expelling. (71:19) And God made for you the earth as a carpet (71:20) that you may thread in it ways through ravines.

Chapter 72 The Jinn 5 Signs

(72:3) Truly He, exalted be the grandeur of our Lord. He has taken no companion (f) to Himself nor a son

(72:25) Say: I am not informed if what you are promised is near, or if my Lord will assign for it a space of time. (72:26) He is The One Who has Knowledge of the unseen! And He discloses not the unseen to anyone, (72:27) but a Messenger with whom He is content. Then truly He dispatches in advance of him and from behind him a watcher (72:28) that he may know that they have expressed the messages of their Lord. He comprehends whatever is with them and He counts everything with numbers.

Chapter 75 The Resurrection 4 Signs

(75:36) Assumes the human being that he will be left aimless? (75:37) Was he not a sperm-drop that is spilled from seminal fluids? (75:38) After that he had been a clot and He created him and shaped him. (75:39) Then He made of him two sexes, the male and the female. (75:40) Is not that One Who has the Power to give life to the dead?

Chapter 76 The Human Being 3 Signs

(76:1) Has there approached the human being a long course of time when he was nothing remembered? (76:2) Truly We made the human being of a mingling of seminal fluids that We may test him. So We made him hearing, seeing. (76:3) Truly We have guided him on the way, whether he be one who is thankful or unthankful.

Chapter 77 The Ones Who Are Sent 8 Signs

(77:20) Have We not created you of despicable water? (77:21) Then We made it in a secure stopping place (77:22) for a known measuring? (77:23) And We measured. How bountiful are the ones who measure! (77:24) Woe on that day to the ones who deny! (77:25) Have We not made the earth a place of drawing together (77:26) the living and the lifeless? (77:27) We made on it soaring, firm mountains. We satiated you with the sweetest kind of water.

Chapter 78 The Tiding 16 Signs

(78:1) About what demand you of one another? (78:2) Of the sublime tiding (78:3) about which they are ones who are at variance in it? (78:4) No indeed! Truly they will know. (78:5) After that, no indeed, truly they will know. (78:6) Have We not made the earth for a cradling (78:7) and the mountains as stakes? (78:8) And have We not created you in pairs (78:9) and We made your sleep as a rest. (78:10) And We made the nighttime as a garment. (78:11) And We made the daytime for you to earn a living. (78:12) And We have built over you seven superior ones. (78:13) And We made a bright, light-giving lamp. (78:14) And We sent forth clouds bringing rain, water cascading, (78:15) with which We bring forth grain and plants (78:16) and luxuriant Gardens.

Chapter 80 He Frowned 16 Signs

(80:17) Perdition to the human being! How ungrateful he is! (80:18) From what thing has He created him? (80:19) He created him from seminal fluids then determined that he be. (80:20) He made the way easy for him after that. (80:21) Then He causes him to die and after that to be buried. (80:22) Then when He willed, He will revive him. (80:23) No indeed! The human being has not finished what He had commanded him. (80:24) Then let the human being look on his food— (80:25) how We truly unloosed rain water with a pouring out. (80:26) After that We split the earth, a splitting. (80:27) And We put forth in it grain (80:28) and grapevines and reeds(80:29) and olives and date palm trees (80:30) and dense orchards (80:31) and sweet fruits and whatever grows on the earth, (80:32) an enjoyment for you and your flocks.

Chapter 82 The Splitting Apart 3 Signs

(82:6) O human being! What has deluded thee as to thy generous Lord, (82:7) He Who created thee, then shaped thee in proportion. (82:8) He composed thee in whatever form He willed.

Chapter 85 The Constellations 5 Signs

(85:12) Truly the seizing by force by thy Lord is severe. (85:13) Truly He causes to begin and He causes to bring back. (85:14) He is the The Forgiving, The Loving, (85:15) the Possessor of the Glorious Throne (85:16) Who achieves what He wants.

Chapter 86 The Night Visitor 6 Stars

(86:5) So let the human being look on of what he was created. (86:6) He was created of water, that which gushes forth, (86:7) going forth from between the loins and the breast bone. (86:8) Truly He, in returning him, is One Who has the Power. (86:9) On a Day all secret thoughts will be tried, (86:10) then there will not be for him any strength nor one who helps.

Chapter 87 The Lofty 5 Signs

(87:1) Glorify the Name of thy Lord, The Lofty (87:2) Who created and shaped (87:3) and who ordained and then guided (87:4) and who brought out the pasture (87:5) then made it dark colored refuse.

Chapter 88 The Overwhelming Event 4 Signs

(88:17) Will they not then look on the camel, how it was created? (88:18) And of the heaven, how it was lifted up? (88:19) And the mountains, how they were hoisted up? (88:20) And the earth, how it was stretched out?

Chapter 90 The Land 3 Signs

(90:8) Have We not made two eyes for him (90:9) and a tongue and two lips (90:10) and guided him to the two open highways?

Chapter 91 The Sun 4 Ruby Signs 3 Pearl Signs

(91:1) Rubies and Pearls: By the sun and its forenoon (91:2) and by the moon when it relates to it (91:3) and by the daytime when it displays it (91:4) and by the nighttime when it overcomes it (91:5) and by the heaven and what built it (91:6) and by the earth and what widened it

Chapter 96 The Blood Clot 8 Signs

(96:1) Recite in the Name of thy Lord Who created. (96:2) He created the human being from a clot. (96:3) Recite: Thy Lord is the Most Generous, (96:4) He Who taught by the pen. (96:5) He taught the human being what he knows not. (96:6)

No indeed! The human being is truly defiant. (96:7) He considers himself to be one who is self-sufficient. (96:8) Truly to thy Lord is the return.

Chapter 112 The Sincere Expression

(112:1) Say: He is The God, One (112:2) God, the Everlasting Refuge. (112:3) He has neither procreated nor was He to be procreated (112:4) and there is nothing comparable to Him.

Part 3: The Pearls of the Quran

The Pearls are the signs which describe the straight path and the signs which urge the human being to follow it. There are 741 signs of Pearls in the Quran. This is the practical part.

Chapter 2 :The Cow 46 Signs

(2:1) Alif Lām Mīm. (2:2) That is the Book—there is no doubt in it, a guidance for the ones who are Godfearing: (2:3) Those who believe in the unseen and perform the formal prayer. And they spend out of what We have provided for them (2:4) and those who believe in what was sent forth to thee and what was sent forth before thee and they are certain of the world to come. (2:5) Those are on a guidance from their Lord; and those, they are the ones who prosper.

(2:21) O humanity! Worship your Lord Who created you and those who were before you so that perhaps you would become Godfearing.

(2:40) O Children of Israel! Remember My divine blessing with which I was gracious to you and live up to the compact with Me. I will live up to the compact with you. And have reverence for Me alone. (2:41) And believe in what I have sent forth, that which establishes as true what is with you. And be not the first one who is ungrateful for it; and exchange not My signs for a little price. And be Godfearing of Me alone. (2:42) And confuse not The Truth with falsehood nor keep back The Truth while you know. (2:43) And perform the formal prayer and give the purifying alms and bow down with the ones who bow down. (2:44) You command humanity to virtuous conduct and you yourselves forget while you recount the Book? Will you not then be reasonable? (2:45) And pray for help with patience and formal prayer. And truly it is arduous but for the ones who are humble.

(2:74) Then your hearts became hard after that so that they were as rocks or harder in hardness. And truly of the rocks there are some that rivers gush forth from them. And truly there are some that split open so water goes forth from them. And truly there are some that crash down, dreading God, and God is not One Who is Heedless of what you do. (2:75) Are you desirous that they should believe in you while surely a group of people among them had been hearing the assertion of God and then after that they would tamper with it after they had discerned it, while they know?

(2:83) . . . . and speak with kindness to humanity and perform the formal prayer and give the purifying alms. After that you turned away but a few among you, you were ones who turned aside.

(2:112) Yea! Whoever has submitted his face to God and he is one who is a doer of good, then for him his compensation is with his Lord. And there will be neither fear in them, nor will they feel remorse.

(2:152) So remember Me and I will remember you. And give thanks to (2:153) O those who have believed! Pray for help with patience and formal prayer. Truly God is with the ones who remain steadfast. (2:154) And say not about those who were slain in the way of God: They are lifeless. Nay! They are living, except you are not aware. (2:155) We will certainly try you with something of fear and hunger and diminution of wealth and lives and fruits, and give good tidings to the ones who remain steadfast, (2:156) those who, when an affliction lighted on them, they said: Truly we belong to God, and truly we are ones who return to Him. (2:157) Those are they on whom blessings will be sent from their Lord and mercy; and those, they are the ones who are truly guided.

(2:168) O humanity! Eat of what is in and on the earth —

lawful, wholesome— and follow not the steps of the Satan. Truly he is a clear enemy to you. (2:169) Truly he commands you to evil and depravity and that you say about God what you know not.

(2:177) It is not virtuous conduct that you turn your faces towards the East or the West. Rather virtuous conduct consists of: Whoever has believed in God and the Last Day and the angels and the Book and the Prophets. And whoever gives wealth out of cherishing Him to the kin and to the orphans and to the needy and to the traveler of the way and for one who seeks and freeing a bondsperson and whoever performs the formal prayer and gives the purifying alms and ones who lives up to their compact when they made a contract; and the ones who remain steadfast in desolation and tribulation and at the time of danger, those, they are sincere; and those, they are the ones who are Godfearing!

(2:194) Fight aggression in the Sacred Month for the Sacred Month and so reciprocation for all sacred things. So whoever commits aggression against you, commit aggression against him likewise as he has committed aggression against you. And be Godfearing of God and know God is with the ones who are Godfearing. (2:195) And spend in the way of God, and cast not yourselves by your own hands into deprivation by fighting. And do good. Truly God loves the ones who are doers of good.

(2:218) Truly those who have believed and those who have emigrated and have struggled in the way of God, those have hope for the mercy of God. And God is Forgiving, Compassionate.

(2:235) . . . . And know that God knows what is within yourselves. So be fearful of Him. And know that God is Forgiving, Forbearing.

(2:261) A parable of those who spend their wealth in the way of God is like a parable of a grain. It puts forth seven ears of wheat. In every ear of wheat, a hundred grains, and God multiplies for whom He wills, and God is One Who Embraces, Knowing. (2:262) Those who spend their wealth in the way of God, and after that pursue not what they spent with reproachful reminders nor injury, the compensation for them is with their Lord. And there will be neither fear in them nor will they feel remorse.

(2:278) O those who have believed! Be Godfearing of God and forsake what remains of usury if you have been ones who believe. (2:279) But if you accomplish it not, then take notice of war from God and His Messenger. And if you repent, you will have your principal capital, doing no wrong to others nor will wrong be done to you. (2:280) And if a debtor had been in adversity, then a respite until a time of ease and prosperity. And it is better for you that you be charitable; if you had been knowing. (2:281) And be Godfearing of a Day on which you will be returned to God; after that every soul will be paid its account in full for what it has earned and they will not be done wrong.

(2:284) To God belongs what is in the heavens, and in and on the earth, whether you show what is within yourself, or conceal it, God will make a reckoning with you for it; and He will forgive whom He wills and He will punish whom He wills, and God is Powerful over everything. (2:285) The Messenger believes in what was sent forth to him from his Lord as do the ones who believe. All have believed in God and His angels and His Books and His Messengers saying: We separate and divide not among anyone of His Messengers. And they said: We heard and we obeyed; so grant Thy forgiveness, Our Lord! And to Thee is the Homecoming.

(2:286) God places not a burden on a soul beyond its capacity. For it is what it has earned and against it is what it has deserved, our Lord! Take us not to task if we forget or make a mistake. Our Lord! Load not on us a severe test like that which Thou hast burdened those before us. Our Lord! Burden us not such that we have no power for it; and pardon us and forgive us and have mercy on us. Thou art our Defender so help us against the ungrateful folk.

Chapter 3 The Family of Imran 34 Signs

(3:7) It is He who has sent forth to thee the Book. In it are signs, ones that are definitive. They are the essence of the Book and others, ones that are unspecific; then those whose hearts are swerving, they follow what is unspecific in it, looking for dissent and looking for an interpretation, and none knows its interpretation but God, and the ones who are firmly rooted in knowledge say: We have believed in it as all is from our Lord, and none recollects but those who have intuition. (3:8) Our Lord! Cause our hearts not to swerve after Thou hast guided us and bestow on us mercy from that which proceeds from Thy Presence. Truly Thou, Thou alone art The Giver. (3:9) Our Lord! Truly Thou art One Who Gathers humanity on a Day in which there is no doubt in it. Truly God breaks not His solemn declaration.

(3:14) Was made to appear pleasing to humanity the cherishing of what they have an appetite for: From women and children and heaped up heaps of gold and silver and branded horses and flocks, and tilled land, that is the enjoyment of this present life; while God, with Him is the goodness of the Excellent Abode. (3:15) Say: Shall I tell you of better than that? For those who were Godfearing, with their Lord are Gardens beneath which rivers run. They are ones who will dwell in them forever with purified spouses and contentment from God, and God is Seeing His servants, (3:16) those who say: Our Lord! Truly we have believed, so forgive us our impieties and protect us from the punishment of the fire: (3:17) The ones who remain steadfast and the ones who are sincere and the ones who are morally obligated and the ones who are expenders in the way of God and the ones who ask for forgiveness at the breaking of day.

(3:28) Let not the ones who believe take to themselves the ones who are ungrateful for protectors instead of the ones who believe; and whoever accomplishes that is not with God in anything unless it is because you are Godfearing that you are being cautious toward them, and God cautions you of Himself, and to God is the Homecoming.

(3:31) Say: If you have been loving God, then follow me and God will love you and forgive you your impieties, God is Forgiving, Compassionate. (3:32) Say: Obey God and the Messenger; then if they turn away, then truly God loves not the ones who are ungrateful.

(3:83) Desire they other than the way of life of God while to Him submitted whatever is in the heavens and the earth willingly or unwillingly and they will be returned to Him?

(3:92) You will never attain virtuous conduct until you spend of what you love. And whatever thing you spend, truly God is Knowing of it.

(3:102) O those who have believed! Be Godfearing of God as it is His right that He should be feared and die not but that you be ones who submit to the One God. (3:103) And cleave firmly to the rope of God altogether and be not split up. And remember the divine blessing of God on you when you were enemies. Then He brought your hearts together and you became brothers by His divine blessing and you had been on the brink of an abyss of the fire and He saved you from it, thus God makes manifest to you His signs, so that perhaps you would be truly guided. (3:104) And there may be from among you a community who calls to good and commands to that which is moral, and prohibits that which is immoral.

(3:113) They are not all the same, among the People of the Book is a community of ones who are upstanding. They recount the signs of God in the night watch of the night and they prostrate. (3:114) They believe in God and the Last Day and they command that which is moral and prohibit that which is immoral and they compete with one another in good deeds. Those are among the ones in accord with morality. (3:115) And whatever of good they accomplish will never go unappreciated, and God is Knowing of the ones who are Godfearing. (3:116) Truly those who are ungrateful, never will avail them their wealth nor their children against God at all; and those will be the Companions of the Fire. They, they are ones who will dwell in it forever. (3:117) The parable of what they spend in this present life is like the parable of a freezing wind in it that lights on the cultivation of the folk who did wrong themselves and causes it to perish. And God did not wrong them, but they did wrong themselves.

(3:128) It is none of thy affair at all whether He turns to them in forgiveness or He punishes them. Then truly they are ones who are unjust. (3:129) And to God belongs whatever is in the heavens and whatever is in and on the earth. He forgives whom He wills and punishes whom He wills. And God is Forgiving, Compassionate.

(3:133) And compete with one another for forgiveness from your Lord and for a Garden whose depth is as the heavens and the earth, prepared for the ones who are Godfearing, (3:134) those who spend in gladness and tribulation and who are the ones who choke their rage and the ones who pardon humanity, and God loves the ones who are doers of good. (3:135) And those who, when they commit an indecency or do wrong to themselves, they remember God and then they ask for forgiveness for their impieties —and who forgives impieties but God— and persist not in what impiety they have committed while they know. (3:136) Those, their recompense is forgiveness from their Lord and Gardens beneath which rivers run, ones who will dwell in them forever.

And how bountiful is the compensation for the ones who work!

(3:145) It has not been not for any soul to die but with the permission of God. Prescribed is that which is appointed, and whoever wants a reward for good deeds in the present, We will give him that. And whoever wants a reward for good deeds in the world to come, We will give him that. And We will give recompense to the ones who are thankful.

(3:159) And it is by the mercy of God thou wast gentle with them; and if thou hast been hard, harsh of heart, they would have spread away from around thee; so pardon them, and ask for forgiveness for them, and consult them in the affair; but when thou art resolved, then put thy trust in God. Truly God loves the ones who trust in Him.

(3:180) And assume not those who are misers that what God has given them of His grace is better for them; nay! It is worse for them; to be hung around their necks will be what they were miserly with on the Day of Resurrection, and to God is the heritage of the heavens and the earth, and God is Aware of what you do.

(3:188) Assume not that those who are glad for what they have brought and who love to be praised for what they have not accomplished, then assume not that they will be kept safe from the punishment; and for them, a painful punishment.

(3:200) O those who have believed! Have patience and excel in patience and be steadfast and be Godfearing of God so that perhaps you would prosper.

Chapter 4 The Women 59 Signs

(4:1) O humanity! Be Godfearing of your Lord Who created you from a single soul and from it created its spouse, and from them both disseminated many men and women. And be Godfearing of God through Whom you demand mutual rights of one another and the rights of blood relations. Truly God has been watching over you.

(4:26) God wants to make manifest to you and to guide you to customs of those who were before you and to turn to you in forgiveness, and God is Knowing, Wise. (4:27) And God wants that He turn to you in forgiveness while those who follow their lusts want that you turn against God in a serious deviation. (4:28) God wants to lighten the burden on you. And the human being was created weak.

(4:31) If you avoid major sins that you are prohibited, We will absolve you of your minor sins and cause you to enter a generous gate. (4:32) And covet not what God has given as advantage of it to some of you over others. For men is a share of what they deserve; and for women is a share of what they (f) deserve. And ask God for His grace, truly God has been Knowing of everything.

(4:36) And worship God and make nothing a partner with Him; and be kind to the ones who are your parents and to kin and the orphans and the needy and to the neighbor who is a stranger and the neighbor who is kin and to the companion by your side and the traveler of the way and whom your right hands possess, truly God loves not ones who have been proud, boastful, (4:37) those who are misers and command humanity to miserliness and keep back what God has given them of His grace, and We have made ready for the ones who are ungrateful a despised punishment (4:38) and those who spend their wealth to show off to humanity and believe neither in God nor in the Last Day, and to whomever Satan is a comrade then how evil a comrade! (4:39) And what would be for them had they believed in God and the Last Day and spent out of what God has provided them? God has been Knowing of them. (4:40) Truly God does not wrong even the weight of an atom; and if there is benevolence, He multiplies it and gives that which proceeds from His Presence a sublime compensation. (4:41) How then will it be when We have brought about from each community a witness and We have brought thee about as witness against these?

(4:48) Truly God forgives not that any partner be made with Him and He forgives other than that whomever He wills. And whoever ascribes partners unto God, then surely he has devised a serious sin. (4:49) Hast thou not seen those who make themselves seem pure? Nay! God makes pure whom He wills. Wrong will not be done to them in the least.

(4:58) Truly God commands you to give back trusts to the people. And when you give judgment between humanity, give judgment justly. Truly how excellent God admonishes you of it, truly God has been Hearing, Seeing.
(4:59) O those who have believed! Obey God and obey the Messenger and those having authority among you; then if you contend with one another in anything, refer it to God and the Messenger if you have been believing in God and the Last Day. That is better and a fairer interpretation.

(4:64) And never have We sent a Messenger, but he is obeyed with the permission of God. And if when they do wrong themselves, they draw near to thee and ask for the forgiveness of God and the Messenger asks for forgiveness for them. They will find God Accepter of Repentance, Compassionate. (4:65) But no! By thy Lord! They will not believe until they make thee a judge in what they have disagreed about. After that they find within themselves no impediment to what thou hast decided and resign themselves to submission, full submission.

(4:69) And whoever obeys God and the Messenger, those are to whom God has been gracious among the Prophets and just persons and the witnesses and the ones who are in accord with morality. And excellent are those as allies! (4:70) That is the grace from God. And God has sufficed as Knowing.

(4:79) Whatever of benevolence lights on thee is from

God; and whatever evil deeds light on thee then is from thyself. And We have sent thee to humanity as a Messenger. And God has sufficed as Witness. (4:80) Whoever obeys the Messenger has surely obeyed God; and whoever turns away, then We have not sent thee as a guardian over them. (4:81) And they say: Obedience! Then when they depart from thee, a section of them spend the night planning on other than what thou sayest; and God records what they spend the night planning; so turn aside from them, and put thy trust in God. And God has sufficed as Trustee. (4:82) But no! They meditate not on the Recitation. And had it been from other than God, certainly they would have found in it many contradictions. (4:83) Whenever draws near them a command of security or fear, they broadcast it; and had they referred it to the Messenger, and to those having authority among them, they would have known it, those who investigate from among them, and had it not been for the grace of God on you and His mercy, certainly you would have followed Satan, but a few.

(4:85) Whoever intercedes with a benevolent intercession, he will have for himself a share of it; and whoever intercedes with an intercession for bad deeds, he will have for himself a like part of it, and God has been over everything One Who Oversees. (4:86) And when you were given greetings, then give greetings fairer than that or return the same to them, truly God has been over everything a Reckoner. (4:87) God, there is no god but He. He will certainly gather you on the Day of Resurrection; there is no doubt about it, and who is one who is more sincere in discourse than God?

(4:94) O those who have believed! When you travel in the way of God, then become clear and say not to whomever gives you a proposal of peace: Thou art not one who believes, looking for advantage in this present life. With God is much gain. Thus you had been before like this. Then God showed grace to you so become clear. Truly God has been Aware of what you do. (4:95) Not on the same level are the ones who sit at home among the ones who believe —other than those who are disabled— and the ones who struggle in the way of God with their wealth and their lives. God has given advantage to the ones who struggle with their wealth and their lives by a degree over the ones who sit at home. And to each God has promised fairness. And God has given advantage to the ones who struggle over the ones who sit at home with a sublime compensation, (4:96) degrees from Him and forgiveness and mercy. And God has been Forgiving, Compassionate.

(4:103) Then when you have satisfied the formal prayer, then remember God when upright and sitting and on your sides. And then when you are secure, perform the formal prayer. Truly the formal prayer has been —for the ones who believe— a timed prescription. (4:104) And be not feeble in looking for the folk; if you are suffering, they are suffering as you are suffering; yet you hope from God what they hope not for, and God has been Knowing, Wise. (4:105) Truly We have sent forth to thee the Book with The Truth so that thou shalt give judgment among humanity by what God has caused thee to see. And be thou not an adversary for ones who are traitors. (4:106) And ask God for forgiveness; truly God has been Forgiving, Compassionate. (4:107) And dispute not for those who are dishonest to themselves. Truly God loves not anyone who has been a sinful betrayer.

(4:110) And whoever does evil or does wrong to himself and after that asks for forgiveness from God will truly find God Forgiving, Compassionate. (4:111) And whoever earns a sin, truly he earns it only against himself. And God has been Knowing, Wise. (4:112) And whoever earns a transgression or a sin and after that accuses an innocent one has surely laid a burden on himself of false charges that harm another's reputation and a clear sin. (4:113) And were it not for the grace of God on thee and His mercy, a section of them would do something that would cause thee to go astray. And they caused none to go astray but themselves; and they injured thee not at all. And God has sent forth the Book to thee and wisdom and has taught thee what thou hast not known. The grace of God has been sublime upon thee. (4:114) No good is there in most of their conspiring secretly but for him who commands charity or one who is honorable or makes things right between humanity. And whoever accomplishes that — looking for the good pleasure of God— then We will give him a sublime compensation. (4:115) And whoever makes a breach with the Messenger after the guidance has become clear to him and follows a way other than that of the ones who believe, We will turn him away from what he has turned to and We will scorch him in hell; and how evil a Homecoming! (4:116) Truly God forgives not that any partner be ascribed to Him. And He forgives other than that whomever He wills. And whoever makes partners with God, then surely goes astray, a wandering far astray.

(4:125) And who is fairer in the way of life than he who has submitted his face to God, and he is one who is a doer of good and follows the creed of Abraham, a monotheist, and God took Abraham to Himself as a friend. (4:126) And to God is whatever is in the heavens and whatever is in and on the earth. And God has been One Who Encloses everything.

(4:129) You will never be able to be just between wives, even if you are eager; so incline not with total inclination away from her, forsaking her as if she be one who is in suspense. And if you make things right and are Godfearing, then truly God has been Forgiving, Compassionate.

(4:146) but those who repented and made things right and cleaved firmly to God and made sincere their way of life for God, then those will be with the ones who believe; and

God will give the ones who believe a sublime compensation. (4:147) What would God accomplish by your punishment if you have given thanks to Him and have believed in Him? God has been One Who is Responsive, Knowing. (4:148) God loves not the open publishing of evil sayings except by him who had been wronged. God has been Hearing, Knowing. (4:149) If you show good or conceal it or pardon evil, then truly God has been Pardoning, Powerful.

(4:162) But the ones who are firmly rooted in knowledge among them and the ones who believe, they believe in what was sent forth to thee and what was sent forth before thee. They are the ones who perform the formal prayer. And they are the ones who give the purifying alms and they are the ones who believe in God and the Last Day. It is those to whom We will give a sublime compensation.

(4:174) O humanity! Surely there has drawn near to you proof from your Lord. And We have sent forth to you a clear light. (4:175) So for those who have believed in God and cleave firmly to Him, then He will cause them to enter into mercy from Him and grace, and guide them to Himself on a straight path.

Chapter 5 The Table Spread with Food 12 Signs

(5:2) O those who have believed! Profane not the way-marks of God nor the Sacred Month nor the sacrificial gift nor the garlanded nor the ones who are bound for the Sacred House looking for grace from their Lord and contentment. And when you have left your pilgrim sanctity, then hunt. And let not that you detest a folk that barred you from the Masjid al-Haram that you be moved to commit aggression. And cooperate with one another in virtuous conduct and God-consciousness; and cooperate not with one another in sin and deep seated dislike. And be Godfearing of God; truly God is Severe in repayment. (5:3) Forbidden to you was carrion and blood and flesh of swine and what of it was hallowed to other than God and the strangled beast and one that has been beaten to death and one that has fallen to its death and one gored to death and one eaten by a beast of prey —but what you slaughter lawfully— and those slaughtered to fetishes and those you partition by divining arrows. That is disobedience, today those who are ungrateful have given up hope because of your way of life. So dread them not but dread Me. Today I have perfected your way of life for you and I have fulfilled My divine blessing on you and I am well-pleased with submission to the One God for your way of life. Then whoever is driven by necessity due to famine, not one who is inclining to sin, then truly God is Forgiving, Compassionate.

(5:8) O those who have believed! Be the ones who are staunch as witnesses in equity for God; and let not that you detest a folk move you that you deal not justly. Be just, that is nearer to God-consciousness and be Godfearing of God. Truly God is Aware of what you do. And God has promised those who have believed and the ones who have acted in accord with morality that for them is forgiveness and a sublime compensation.

(5:35) O those who have believed! Be Godfearing of God and be looking for an approach to Him and struggle in His way so that perhaps you would prosper.

(5:49) And give judgment between them by what God has sent forth and follow not their desires and beware of them so that they tempt thee not from some of what God has sent forth to thee; and if they turn away, then know that God only wants that He light on them for some of their impieties, and truly many within humanity are ones who disobey. (5:50) Are they looking for a determination of ignorance? And who is more fair than God in determination for a folk who are certain?

(5:83) And when they heard what was sent forth to the Messenger, thou hast seen their eyes overflow with tears because they have recognized The Truth; they say: Our Lord! We have believed so write us down with the ones who bear witness. (5:84) And why should we not have believed in God and in what has drawn near to us of The Truth? And we are desirous that Our Lord would cause us to enter the Garden among the folk— the ones who are in accord with morality. (5:85) Then God repaid them for what they said— Gardens beneath which rivers run, ones who will dwell in them forever. And that is the recompense of the ones who are doers of good.

(5:93) There is not for those who have believed and the ones who have acted in accord with morality blame for what they have tasted as long as they were Godfearing and have believed and are the ones who have acted in accord with morality and after that they were Godfearing and have believed. And after that they were Godfearing and did good, and God loves the ones who are doers of good.

(5:105) O those who have believed! Upon you is the charge of your souls; one who goes astray injures you not if you are truly guided. To God is the return of you all. Then He will tell you what you had been doing.

Chapter 6 The Flocks 17 Signs

(6:32) And this present life is nothing but a pastime and diversion, and the Last Abode is better for those who are Godfearing, will you not then be reasonable?

(6:44) So when they forgot about what they were reminded in it, We opened to them the doors of everything. Until when they were glad with what they were given, We suddenly took them. Lo and behold! They were ones seized with despair. (6:45) So cut off were the last remnant of the folk who did wrong. And The Praise belongs to God, Lord of the worlds.

(6:52) And drive not away those who call to their Lord in the morning after the formal prayer and the evening, wanting His Countenance; their reckoning is not on thee at all. And thy reckoning is not on them at all. Shouldst thou drive them away, then thou wouldst become of the ones who are unjust. (6:53) Even so We tried some of them by others that they should say: Are those the ones to whom God has shown grace from among us, is not God greater in knowledge of the ones who are thankful? (6:54) And when draw near to thee, those who believe in Our signs say: Peace be to you; your Lord has prescribed mercy for Himself; so that anyone of you who did evil in ignorance then repented afterwards and makes things right, then truly He is Forgiving, Compassionate.

(6:68) And when thou seest those who are engaged in idle talk about Our signs, then turn aside from them until they discuss in conversation other than that. And if Satan should cause thee to forget, then after a reminder, sit not with the folk, the ones who are unjust. (6:69) There is not on those who are Godfearing, anything of their reckoning but a reminder so that perhaps they would be Godfearing.

(6:82) Those who have believed and have not confused their belief with injustice, those, to them belongs the place of sanctuary. And they are ones who are truly guided.

(6:120) And forsake manifest sin and its inward part. Truly those who earn sin, they will be given recompense for what they had been gaining.

(6:125) And whomever God wants, He guides him. He expands his breast for The Submission to One God; and whomever He wants to cause to go astray, He makes his breast tight, narrow as if he had been climbing up a difficult ascent. Thus God assigns disgrace on those who believe not. (6:126) And this is the straight path of thy Lord, surely We have explained distinctly the signs for a folk who recollect.

(6:127) For them is the abode of peace with their Lord; and He is their protector for what they had been doing.

(6:151) Say: Approach now; I will recount what your Lord has forbidden you; that you not make any partner with Him at all; and to the ones who are your parents, kindness; and kill not your children from want; We will provide for you and for them; and come not near any indecencies whether these be manifest or what is inward; and kill not a soul which God has forbidden unless rightfully. That He has charged you with so that perhaps you would be reasonable. (6:152) And come not near the property of the orphan but with what is fairer until one reaches maturity and comes of age; and live up to the full measure and balance with equity; We will not place a burden on any soul but to its capacity; and when you have said something, be just, even if be with kin; and live up to the compact of God. This He has charged you with it so that perhaps you would recollect. (6:153) And that this is My straight path, so follow it; and follow not the ways that will split you up from His way. This He has charged you of it so that perhaps you would be Godfearing.

(6:160) Whoever draws near with benevolence, then for him, ten times the like of it; and whoever draws near with an evil deed, then will not be given recompense but with its like and wrong will not be done to them.

Chapter 7 The Elevated Places 8 Signs

(7:29) Say: My Lord has commanded me to equity; and set your faces at every place of prostration and call to Him ones who are sincere and devoted in the way of life to Him. As He began you, you will revert to Him. (7:30) A group of people He guided and a group of people realized their fallacy, truly they took satans to themselves as protectors instead of God and they assume that they are ones who were truly guided. (7:31) O Children of Adam! Take your adornment at every place of prostration and eat and drink, but exceed not all bounds. Truly He loves not the ones who are excessive.

(7:96) And if the people of the towns believed and were Godfearing, We would have opened blessings for them from the heaven and the earth except they denied. So We took them for what they had been earning.

(7:165) So when they forgot about what they were reminded, We rescued those who prohibited evil and We took those who did wrong with a terrifying punishment because they had been disobedient.

(7:203) And when thou approached them not with a sign, they said: Why hast thou not improvised one? Say: I follow only what is revealed to me from my Lord. This is clear evidence from your Lord and guidance and mercy for a folk who believe. (7:204) And when the Quran is recited, listen to it and pay heed so that perhaps you would find mercy. (7:205) And remember thy Lord in thyself humbly and with awe instead of openly publishing the sayings at the first part of the day and the eventide. And be thou not among the ones who are heedless. (7:206) Truly those who are with thy Lord grow not arrogant from His worship and they glorify Him and they prostrate themselves to Him.

Chapter 8 The Spoils of War 11 Signs

(8:1) They ask thee about the spoils of war; say: The spoils of war belong to God and the Messenger; so be Godfearing of God and make things right among you; and obey God and his Messenger if you have been ones who believe. (8:2) The ones who believe are only those whose hearts quake when God was remembered. When His signs were recounted to them, their belief increases and they put their trust in the Lord. (8:3) They are those who perform the formal prayer and spend out of what We have provided them.

(8:4) Those, they are the ones who truthfully believe. There are for them degrees with their Lord and forgiveness and generous resources,

(8:24) O those who have believed! Respond to God and to the Messenger when He calls you to what gives you life; and know truly that God comes between a man and his heart and that to Him you will be assembled. (8:25) Be Godfearing of a test which will not light on those of you who did wrong particularly; and know that God is truly Severe in repayment. (8:26) And remember when you were few, taken advantage of because of your weakness on the earth. You feared humanity would snatch you away so He gave you refuge and confirmed you with His help and provided you with what is good so that perhaps you would give thanks. (8:27) O those who have believed! Betray not God and the Messenger nor betray your trusts when you know. (8:28) And know that your wealth and your children are a test and that God, with Him is a sublime compensation.

(8:53) That is because God will never alter a divine blessing when He has been gracious to a folk until they alter what is within themselves and truly God is Hearing, Knowing.

Chapter 9 Repentance 12 Signs

(9:18) Only he frequents places of prostration to God who believes in God and the Last Day, and performs the formal prayer and gives the purifying alms and dreads none but God; perhaps those are to be among the ones who are truly guided.

(9:24) Say: If had been your fathers and your sons and your brothers and your spouses and your kinspeople and the wealth you have gained and the transactions you dread may slacken and the dwellings with which you are well-pleased more beloved to you than God and His Messenger and struggling in His Way, then await until God brings His command, and God guides not the folk, ones who disobey.

(9:38) O those who have believed! What is it with you when it is said to you: Move forward in the way of God, you incline heavily downwards to the earth? Are you so well-pleased with this present life instead of the world to come? But the enjoyment of this present life is nothing but little compared to the world to come.

(9:71) The ones who are male believers and the ones who are female believers, some are protectors of the other. They command to that which is moral and they prohibit that which is immoral and they perform the formal prayer and give the purifying alms and obey God and His Messenger. Those, God will have mercy on them, truly God is Almighty, Wise.

(9:100) As for the foremost ones who outstrip among the ones who emigrate and the helpers and those who followed them in kindness, God is well-pleased with them and they are well-pleased with Him. He has prepared for them Gardens beneath which rivers run, ones who will dwell in them forever, eternally. That is the winning the sublime triumph. (9:104) Know they not that God is He Who accepts remorse from His servants and takes charities and that God, He is The Accepter of Repentance, The Compassionate? (9:105) And say: Act! God will consider your actions and so will His Messenger and the ones who believe; and you will be returned to Him, One Who has Knowledge of the unseen and the visible. Then He will tell you what you had been doing.

(9:111) Truly God has bought from the ones who believe themselves and their properties for the Garden is theirs! They fight in the way of God so they kill and are slain; it is a promise rightfully on Him in the Torah and the Gospel and the Quran. And who is more true to His compact than God? Then rejoice in the good tidings of the bargain that you made in the trade with Him. And that, it is the winning the sublime triumph (9:112) for the repentant worshippers, the ones who praise, the ones who are inclined to fast, the ones who bow down, the ones who prostrate themselves, the ones who command that which was moral and the ones who prohibit that which was immoral, and the ones who guard the ordinances of God, and give good tidings to the ones who believe!

(9:122) And it has not been for the ones who believe to move forward collectively. If every band not move forward of them but a section of people only, it may be that they become learned in the way of life and that they may warn their folk when they return to them so that perhaps they would beware?

(9:128) Certainly there has drawn near you a Messenger from among yourselves. It is grievous to him that you fall into misfortune; he is anxious for you and to the ones who believe, gentle, compassionate. (9:129) But if they turn away, say: God is enough for me. There is no god but He; in Him I put my trust; and He is the Lord of the Sublime Throne.

Chapter 10 Jonah 18 Signs

(10:7) Truly those who hope not for their meeting with Us, but are well-pleased with this present life and are secure in it and those who are of ones who are heedless of Our signs. (10:8) Those, their place of shelter will be the fire because of what they had been earning. (10:9) Truly those who have believed and the ones who have acted in accord with morality, their Lord will guide them in their belief; rivers will run beneath them in Gardens of Bliss. (10:10) They will call out from it: Glory be to Thee, O God! And their greetings in it will be: Peace! And the last of their calling out will be that the Praise belongs to God the Lord of the worlds!

(10:22) He it is Who sets you in motion through dry land and the sea; until when you have been in boats and they run them with the good wind and they are glad in it. A wind storm draws near to them. Waves draw near from every place, and they think that they were enclosed by it. They call to God, ones who are sincere and devoted in their way of life to Him saying: If Thou wert to rescue us from this, we would certainly be of the ones who are thankful. (10:23) But when He rescues them, lo and behold! They are insolent in and on the earth without right, O humanity, your insolence is only against yourselves; an enjoyment of this present life; after that to Us is your return then We will tell you what you had been doing. (10:24) The parable of this present life is but like water that We send forth from heaven. It mingles with the plants of the earth —from which you eat—humanity and flocks— until when the earth takes its ornaments and is decorated and its people thought that truly they were the ones who had the power over it! Our command approaches it by nighttime or by daytime. Then We make it stubble as if it had not flourished yesterday. Thus We explain distinctly the signs for a folk who reflect. (10:25) And God calls to the Abode of Peace and He guides whom He wills to a straight path. (10:26) For those who have done good is the fairest and increase; neither will gloom come over their faces nor abasement. Those are the Companions of the Garden; they, ones who will dwell in it forever.

(10:55) No doubt to God belongs all that is in the heavens and the earth, no doubt the promise of God is true, but most of them know not. (10:56) It is He Who gives life and causes to die and to Him you will return. (10:57) O humanity! Surely an admonishment has drawn near to you from your Lord and a healing for what is in the breasts and a guidance and a mercy for ones who believe. (10:58) Say: In the grace of God and in His mercy therein let them be glad. That is better than what they gather.

(10:62) No doubt with the faithful friends of God there

will be neither fear in them, nor will they feel remorse. (10:63) Those who have believed and are Godfearing, (10:64) for them are good tidings in this present life and in the world to come. There is no substitution for the Words of God. This is the winning the sublime triumph. (10:65) And let not their saying grieve thee. Truly all great glory belongs to God. He is The Hearing, The Knowing.

Chapter 11 Hud 20 Signs

(11:1) Alif Lām Rā . A Book, the signs in it were set clear. After that they were explained distinctly from that which proceeds from the Presence of the Wise, Aware, (11:2) that you not worship any but God. Truly I am a warner to you from Him and a bearer of good tidings (11:3) and that you ask for forgiveness from your Lord. After that repent to Him that He may give you fair enjoyment for a term, that which was determined. He gives His grace to every owner of grace; and if they turn away, I fear for you the punishment of a Great Day.

(11:9) And if We cause the human being to experience mercy from Us and after that tear it out from him, truly he, he becomes hopeless, ungrateful. (11:10) And if We cause him to experience favor after tribulation has afflicted him, he is certain to say: Evil deeds have gone from me! Truly he becomes glad, boastful. (11:11) But those who have endured patiently and the ones who have acted in accord with morality, those, for them is forgiveness and a great compensation.

(11:14) If they respond not to you, then know that it was only sent forth by the knowledge of God and that there is no god but He; will you then be ones who submit? (11:15) Whoever had been wanting this present life and its adornment, We will pay their account in full to them for their actions in it and they will not be diminished in it. (11:16) Those, there is nothing for them in the world to come but fire; and what they have crafted there has been fruitless and what they had been doing is useless.

(11:61) And We sent to Thamud their brother Salih. He said: O my folk! Worship God. You have no god other than He; He caused you to grow from the earth and settled you on it. so ask for His forgiveness. After that repent to Him. Truly my Lord is Near, One Who Answers.

(11:84) And We sent to Midian their brother Shuayb. He said: O my folk! Worship God. You have no god other than He. And reduce not the measuring vessel and balance. Truly I consider you as good and truly I fear for you the punishment of an Enclosing Day. (11:85) And O my folk! Live up to the measuring vessel and balance in equity; and diminish not of humanity their things, and do no mischief in and on the earth as ones who make corruption. (11:86) What is left by God is best for you if you have been ones who believe. And I am not a Guardian over you. (11:87) They said: O Shuayb! Is it that thy formal prayer commands thee that we should leave what our fathers worship or that we should not accomplish with our possibilities whatever we will; truly thou art the forbearing, the well-intentioned.

(11:110) And certainly We gave Moses the Book, but they were at variance about it. And had it not been for a Word preceding from thy Lord, it would have been decided between them. And truly they were uncertain about it, ones whose suspicions were aroused. (11:111) And truly to each the account will be paid in full by thy Lord for their actions. Truly He is Aware of what they do. (11:112) So go straight as thou wert commanded and those who repent with thee and be not defiant. Truly He is Seeing of what you do. (11:113) Then incline not to those who do wrong so the fire afflict you and there will not be for you any protectors other than God. After that you will not be helped. (11:114) And perform the formal prayer at the two ends of the daytime and at nearness of the nighttime. Truly benevolence causes evil deeds to be put away. That is a reminder for the ones who remember. (11:115) And have patience, for truly God wastes not the compensation of the ones who are doers of good.

Chapter 13 Thunder 8 Signs

(13:17) He sent forth water from heaven and it flowed into valleys according to their measure then the flood bears away the froth. And from what they kindle in a fire, looking for glitter or sustenance, there is a froth the life of it. Thus God compares the Truth and falsehood. Then as for the froth, it goes as swelling while what profits humanity abides on th earth. Thus God propounds parables. (13:18) For those who responded to their Lord, there is the fairest. And for those who respond not to Him, if they had all that is in and on the earth and its like with it, they would offer it as ransom. Those, for them will be a dire reckoning and their place of shelter will be hell. How miserable a cradling. (13:19) Then is he who knows what has been sent forth to thee from thy Lord to be The Truth like he who is unwilling to see? It is only those who have intuition who recollect. (13:20) Those who live up to their compact with God and break not their solemn promise (13:21) and those who reach out to what God has commanded to be joined and dread their Lord and they fear the dire reckoning (13:22) and those who endured patiently, looking for the Countenance of their Lord and who performed the formal prayers and spent out of what We have provided them in secret and in public, and they drive off the evil deed with benevolence —those, for them is the Ultimate Abode:

(13:26) God extends the provision for whom He will and measures it. They are glad in this present life and there is nothing in this present life like the world to come but a brief enjoyment. (13:27) And those who are ungrateful say: Why was a sign not sent forth to him from his Lord, say: Truly

God causes to go astray whom He will and guides to Himself whoever is penitent, (13:28) those who have believed and their hearts are at rest in the remembrance of God, no doubt in the remembrance of God hearts are at rest. (13:29) Those who have believed and the ones who have acted in accord with morality, there is joy for them and a goodness of destination.

Chapter 14 Abraham 6 Signs

(14:24) Hast thou not considered how God has propounded a parable! A good word is like a good tree. Its roots are ones that are firm and its branches are in heaven (14:25) giving its produce at all times with the permission of its Lord, and God propounds parables for humanity so that perhaps they will recollect. (14:26) And the parable of a bad word is that of a bad tree, that was uprooted from above the earth, so it has no stability. (14:27) God makes firm those who have believed with the firm saying in this present life and in the world to come; and God will cause to go astray the ones who are unjust. And God accomplishes what He wills.

(14:38) Our Lord! Truly Thou knowest what we conceal and what we speak openly, and nothing is hidden from God in or on the earth or in heaven. (14:39) The Praise belongs to God Who has bestowed on me in my old age Ishmael and Isaac. And truly my Lord is hearing of all supplication. (14:40) My Lord! Make me one who performs the formal prayer and from my offspring also. Our Lord! Receive my supplication. (14:41) Our Lord! Forgive me and the ones who are my parents and the ones who believe on the Day the reckoning arises.

Chapter 15 The Rocky Tract 6 Signs

(15:85) And We created not the heavens and the earth and all that is in between them but with The Truth, and truly the Hour is one that arrives; so overlook with a sweet over-looking. (15:86) Truly thy Lord is The Knowing Creator. (15:87) And certainly We have given thee seven often re-peated parts of the sublime Quran. (15:88) And stretch not thy eyes at what We have given enjoyment with it to pairs of them, nor feel remorse for them, but make low thy wing to the ones who believe. (15:89) And say: Truly I am a clear warner.

(15:97) And certainly We know that thy breast became narrowed because of what they say. (15:98) So glorify the praises of thy Lord and be of the ones who prostrate them-selves (15:99) and worship thy Lord, until the certainty ap-proaches thee.

Chapter 16 The Bee 14 Signs

(16:61) And if God were to take humanity to task for their injustice, He would not leave on it a moving creature, but He postpones them for a term that was determined; and when their term draws near, neither will they delay it an hour; nor press it forward.

(16:64) And We sent not forth the Book to thee, but that thou mayest make manifest to them those things in which they were at variance in it and as a guidance and a mercy for a folk who believe.

(16:89) On the Day We raise up in every community a witness against them from among themselves; and We will bring thee about as a witness against these. And We have sent down to thee the Book as an exposition that makes everything clear and as a guidance and as a mercy and as good tidings for the ones who submit. (16:90) Truly God commands justice and kindness and giving to ones kin and He prohibits depravity and ones who are immoral and in-solent. He admonishes you so that perhaps you would rec-ollect. (16:91) And live up to the compact of God when you have made a contract. And break not your oaths after ratification, and surely you have made God surety over you. Truly God knows what you accomplish.

(16:96) Whatever is with you will come to an end; and whatever is with God is that which will endure, and We will certainly give recompense to those who endure patiently their fair compensation for what they had been doing. (16:97) Whoever be one who acts in accord with morality, whether male or female, while being one who believes, We will give life—a good life; and We will give recompense to them —their compensation— of the fairest for what they had been doing. (16:98) So when thou recitest the Quran, seek refuge with God from the accursed Satan. (16:99) Truly he has no authority over those who have believed and in their Lord they put their trust. (16:100) His authority is only over those who turn away to him and those, they are ones who are polytheists.

(16:125) Call to the way of your Lord with wisdom and fair admonishment; and dispute with them in a way that is fairer. Truly thy Lord is He Who is greater in knowledge of who has gone astray from His way; and He is greater in knowledge of the ones who are truly guided. (16:126) And if you chastise, then chastise with the like of that with which you were chastised; but if you endure patiently, certainly it is better for ones who remain steadfast. (16:127) And have thou patience and thy patience is only from God. And feel not remorse over them nor be in distress about what they plan. (16:128) Truly God is with those who were Godfearing and those, they are the ones who are doers of good.

Chapter 17 The Journey by Night 29 Signs

(17:23) And thy Lord has decreed that you worship none but Him! And kindness to the ones who are one's parents. If at thy side they reach old age –one of them or both of them–

then say not to them a word of disrespect nor scold them but say a generous saying to them. (17:24) And make thyself low to them, the wing of the sense of humbleness through mercy. And say: O my Lord! Have mercy on them even as they reared me when I was small. (17:25) Your Lord is greater in knowledge of what is within yourselves. If you are ones who are in accord with morality, truly He is Forgiving to those who have been penitent. (17:26) And give to the kin his right, and to the needy and to the traveler of the way and spend not extravagantly an extravagant spending. (17:27) Truly the ones who spent extravagantly have been brothers of the devils; and Satan has been ungrateful to his Lord. (17:28) And if thou turnest aside from them, looking for mercy from thy Lord for which thou hopest, then say to them a saying softly. (17:29) And make not thy hand be one that was restricted to thy neck and extend it not to its utmost expansion so that thou sit as one who is blameworthy, one who was denuded. (17:30) Truly thy Lord extends the provision for whom He wills and He straitens for whom He wills. Truly He, He has been Aware, Seeing of His servants (17:31) And kill not your children in dread of want; We will provide for them and for you. Truly the killing of them has been a grave inequity. (17:32) And come not near committing adultery; truly it has been a great indecency! How evil a way! (17:33) And kill not a soul which God has forbidden, except rightfully, and whoever was slain as one who was treated unjustly, surely We have assigned for his protector, authority, but he should not exceed all bounds in killing; truly he would be one who was helped by the Law. (17:34) And come not near the property of the orphan, but with what is fair until he reaches the coming of age. And live up to the compact; truly the compact has been one that was questioned. (17:35) And live up to the full measure when you measure and weigh with a straight scale. That is best and more fair in interpretation. (17:36) And follow up not of what there is not for thee knowledge of it. Truly having the ability to hear and sight and mind, each of these would be ones that were to be questioned. (17:37) And walk not on the earth exultantly; truly thou shalt never make a hole in the earth and shalt never reach the mountains in height. (17:38) All of that has been bad deeds disliked by thy Lord. (17:39) That is of what thy Lord revealed to thee of wisdom, so set not up with God another god that thou shouldst be cast down into hell as one who is blameworthy, as one who is rejected.

(17:78) Perform the formal prayer from the sinking sun until the darkening of the night and the recital at dawn; truly the dawn recital has been one that was witnessed. (17:79) And keep vigil with it in the night for an unexpected gift for thee. Perhaps thy Lord will raise thee up to a station of one who was praised. (17:80) And say: My Lord! Cause me to enter a gate in sincerity and bring me out as one who was caused to leave in sincerity and assign me from that which proceeds from Thy Presence a helping authority. (17:81) And say: The Truth draws near and falsehood vanishes! Truly falsehood has been made to vanish away. (17:82) We send down in the Quran what is a healing and a mercy for the ones who believe and it increases not the ones who are unjust but in a loss. (17:83) And when We are gracious to the human being, he turns aside and withdraws aside; and when worse afflicts him, he has been hopeless. (17:84) Say: Each does according to his same manner and thy Lord is greater in knowledge of him who is better guided on the way. (17:85) And they will ask thee about the spirit; say: The spirit is of the command of my Lord and you were not given knowledge but a little.

(17:107) Say: Believe in it or believe not. Truly those who were given knowledge before it, when it is recounted to them, they fall down on their visage, ones who prostrate.

(17:108) And they say: Glory be to our Lord! Truly the promise of our Lord has been one that will be accomplished. (17:109) And they fall down on their visages weeping and it increases them in humility. (17:110) Say: Call to God or call to the Merciful; by whatever you call Him, to Him are the Fairest Names. And thou be not loud in thy formal prayer nor speak in a low tone and look for a way between.

Chapter 18 The Cave 19 Signs

(18:28) And have patience thyself with those who call to their Lord after the morning formal prayer and in the evening, wanting His Countenance; and let not thy eyes pass over them wanting the adornment of this present life; and obey not him whose heart We have made neglectful of Our Remembrance and who follows his own desires and whose affair has been all excess.

(18:32) And propound to them the parable of two men: We had assigned to one of them two gardens of grapevines and We had encircled them with date palm trees and We made crops between them. (18:33) Both the gardens gave their produce and failed nothing in the least. We caused a river to gush forth in the midst of them. (18:34) And there had been fruit for him. Then he said to his companion while he was conversing with him: I have more wealth than thee and am mightier with respect to a group of men or jinn. (18:35) And he entered his garden while he was one who was unjust to himself. He said: I think that this will not be destroyed ever. (18:36) And I think that the Hour will not be one that looms near. And if I were to be returned to my Lord, I will surely find better than this as an overturning. (18:37) And his companion said to him while he was conversing with him: Are you ungrateful to Him Who created thee out of earth dust, after that out of seminal fluids, and after that shaped thee into a man? (18:38) Certainly He is God, my

Lord, and I will not make a partner of anyone with my Lord. (18:39) Would that when thou hast entered thy garden thou hadst said: What God willed! There is no strength but with God! If you see I am less than you in wealth and children, (18:40) then perhaps my Lord will give me better than thy garden and will send on it a thunderclap from heaven. Then it will come to be in the morning slippery earth. (18:41) Or it will come to be in the morning that its water will be sinking into the ground so that thou shalt never be able to seek it out. (18:42) And its fruit was enclosed and it came to be in the morning he began turning the palms of his hands around and around for what he had spent on it, while it had fallen in ruins. And he was saying: Would that I had not made anyone partners with my Lord! (18:43) And there was no faction to help him other than God. And he had been one who had been helpless. (18:44) All protection there belongs to God, The Truth. He is Best in rewarding for good deeds and Best in consequence. (18:45) And propound for them the parable of this present life: It is like water that We send forth from heaven and plants of the earth mingle with it and it becomes straw in the morning that winnows in the winds, and God has been everything One Who is Omnipotent. (18:46) Wealth and children are the adornment of this present life; but that which endures are the acts that are in accord with morality. That is better with thy Lord as a reward for good deeds and better for hopefulness.

(18:107) Truly those who have believed and ones who have acted in accord with morality will have a welcome in the Gardens of Paradise, ones who will dwell in them forever. (18:108) They will have no desire for relocation from there. (18:109) Say: If the sea had been ink for the Words of my Lord, the sea would come to an end before the Words of my Lord would come to an end even if We brought about replenishment the like of it. (18:110) Say: I am only a mortal like you. It is revealed to me that your God is One; so whoever has been hoping for the meeting with his Lord, let him be one who acts in accord with morality and makes not a partner —any—in the worship of his Lord.

Chapter 19 Mary 9 Signs

(19:39) And warn them of the Day of Regret when the command will be decided yet they are careless and they believe not. (19:40) Truly We will inherit the earth and whatever is in and on it and to Us they will return.

(19:58) Those are they to whom God has been gracious from among the Prophets of the offspring of Adam and those whom We carried with Noah and of the offspring of Abraham and Israel, Jacob, from among those whom We guided and elected. When were recounted to them the signs of the Merciful they fell down, crying, ones who prostrate themselves. (19:59) Then after them succeeded a succession who wasted the formal prayer and followed their appetites; so they will meet error. (19:60) But those who have repented and have believed and ones who have acted in accord with morality, for those will enter the Garden and wrong will not be done to them in anything.

(19:76) And God increases in guidance those who were truly guided in guidance, and one who endures in accord with morality are better with thy Lord in reward for good deeds and better for turning back.

(19:96) Truly those who have believed and the ones who have acted in accord with morality, The Merciful will assign ardor for them. (19:97) So truly We have made this easy on thy tongue that thou mayest give good tidings with it to the ones who are Godfearing and that thou warnest a most stubborn folk with it. (19:98) How many a generation have We caused to perish before them? Art thou conscious of anyone of them or hear you so much as a whisper from them?

Chapter 20 Ta Ha 19 Signs

(20:13) And I have chosen thee so listen to what is revealed: (20:14) Truly I—I am God; there is no god but Me. So worship Me and perform the formal prayer for My Remembrance. (20:15) Truly the Hour is one that will arrive. I am about to conceal it so that every soul may be given recompense for what it endeavors. (20:16) So let none bar thee from it —whoever believes not in it and follows his own desires—so that thee not survive. (20:17) And what is that in thy right hand O Moses?

(20:72) They said: We will never hold thee in greater favor above the clear portents that have drawn near to us nor above Him Who originated us; so decide whatever thou shalt as one who decides; thou shalt decide not but about this present life. (20:73) For us, truly we have believed in our Lord that He may forgive us our transgressions and what thou hast compelled us to do because of the sorcery, and God is the Best of ones who endure. (20:74) Truly whoever approaches his Lord as one who sins, then truly for him is hell. Neither will he die in it nor will he live. (20:75) And whoever approaches Him as one who believes, surely the one who has acted in accord with morality, for them are lofty degrees,

(20:124) And whoever turns aside from My Remembrance, then truly for him is a livelihood of narrowness. And We will assemble him on the Day of Resurrection unwilling to see. (20:125 He would say: My Lord! Why hast Thou assembled me with the unwilling to see when surely I had been seeing? (20:126) He would say: It is thus: Our signs approached thee, but thou didst forget them; and thus this Day thou shalt be forgotten. (20:127) And thus We give recompense to him who exceeds all bounds and believes not in signs of his Lord. And surely punishment in the world to come is more severe and one that endures. (20:128) Has He guided them not? How many generations have We caused to perish before them amidst whose dwellings they walk, truly in this are signs for the people who have sense. (20:129) And if a Word had not preceded from thy Lord for a term that was determined, it would be close at hand. (20:130) So have patience with what they say and glorify the praises of thy Lord before the coming up of the sun and before sunset; and during the watches of the nighttime and glorify at the end of the daytime, so that perhaps thou wouldst be well-pleasing. (20:131) And stretch not out thy eyes for what We have given of enjoyment to spouses among them as the luster of this present life so that We may try them by it. And provision of thy Lord is best and one that endures. (20:132) And command thy people to the formal prayer, and to maintain patience in it; We ask not of thee for any provision; We provide for thee, and the Ultimate End will be for the God-conscious.

Chapter 21 The Prophets 10 Signs

(21:1) The reckoning for humanity is near while they are ones who turn aside in heedlessness. (21:2) Approaches them not a remembrance from their Lord, one that was renewed, but they listen to it while they play (21:3) being ones whose hearts are diverted, and they kept secret, conspiring secretly those who did wrong. Is this other than a mortal like you; Then will you approach sorcery while you perceive?

(21:105) And certainly We have written down in the Psalms after the Remembrance that the earth will be inherited by My servants —the ones who are in accord with morality. (21:106) Truly in this is the delivering of this message for the folk, ones who worship. (21:107) And We have not sent thee but as a mercy for the worlds. (21:108) Say: It is only revealed to me that your god is only One God; will then you be ones who submit? (21:109) But if they turn away, then say: I have proclaimed to you all equally. And I was not informed whether what you are promised is near or far. (21:110) Truly He knows the openly published saying and He knows what you keep back. (21:111) And I was not informed so that perhaps it would be a test for you and an enjoyment for a while. (21:112) He said: My Lord! Give judgment with The Truth, and our Lord is The Merciful, He Whose help is sought against what you allege.

Chapter 22 The Pilgrimage 15 Signs

(22:11) And among humanity is he who worships God on the fringes; if good lights on him, he is at rest with it; and if a test lights on him, he turns completely over. He loses the present and the world to come. That, it is the clear loss. (22:12) He calls to other than God what neither hurts him nor profits him. That it is a far wandering astray. (22:13) He calls to him whose hurting is nearer than his profiting. How miserable is the defender and how miserable is the acquaintance. (22:14) Truly God will cause to enter those who have believed and the ones who act in accord with morality, Gardens beneath which rivers run. Truly God accomplishes what He wants.

(22:32) That has been commanded! Whoever holds the waymarks of God in honor, then it is, truly from hearts filled with God-consciousness. (22:33) For you in that is what is profitable for a term that which was determined. After that their place of sacrifice is at the Ancient House. (22:34) And for every community We have assigned devotional acts that they may remember the Name of God over what We have provided them of flocks of animals, and your God is One God. Submit to Him, and give good tidings to the ones who humble themselves. (22:35) Those—when God was remembered, their hearts quake and the ones who remain steadfast against whatever may light on them and the ones who perform the formal prayer and who spend out of what We have provided them.

(22:37) Neither their flesh nor their blood attains to God, but your God-consciousness attains Him. Thus He caused them to be subservient to you that you might magnify God in that He has guided you, and give good tidings to the ones who are doers of good. (22:38) Truly God defends those who have believed; truly God loves not anyone who is an ungrateful betrayer.

(22:41) Those who, if We establish them firmly on the earth, they perform the formal prayer and they give the purifying alms and they command to that which is moral and they prohibit that which is immoral, and with God is the Ultimate End of the command.

(22:54) And those who were to be given knowledge know that it is The Truth from thy Lord so that they may believe in it and humble their hearts to Him, and truly God is The One Who Guides those who have believed to a straight path.

(22:77) O those who have believed! Bow down and prostrate yourselves, and worship your Lord, and accomplish good so that perhaps you would prosper. (22:78) And struggle for the sake of God in a true struggling. He has elected you and has not made for you in your way of life any impediment. It is the creed of your father Abraham. It is He Who named you the ones who submit before and in this Recitation so that perhaps the Messenger would be a witness over you and you would be witnesses over humanity. So perform the formal prayer and give the purifying alms and cleave firmly to God. He is your Defender; how excellent a Defender and how excellent a Helper!

Chapter 23 The Believers 22 Signs

(23:1) Surely the ones who believe have prospered, (23:2) those, they who in their formal prayers are ones who are humble; (23:3) and those, they who from idle talk are ones who turn aside; (23:4) and those, they who the purifying alms are ones who do give it; (23:5) and those, they who of their private parts are ones who guard, (23:6) from their spouses or from what their right hands possess. Truly they are ones who are irreproachable. (23:7) Whoever looks for something beyond that, then those, they are the ones who are turning away. (23:8) And those, they who their trusts and their compacts are ones who shepherd. (23:9) And those, they who over their formal prayers are watchful. (23:10) Those, they are ones who will be inheritors, (23:11) those who will inherit Paradise. They are ones who will dwell in it forever.

(23:51) O you Messengers! Eat of what is good and be one who acts in accord with morality. Truly I am Knowing of what you do. (23:52) And truly this community is one community and I am your Lord so be Godfearing. (23:53) Then they cut their affair of unity asunder into sects among themselves, each party glad with what was with them. (23:54) So forsake them for a while in their obstinacy. (23:55) Assume they that with the relief We furnish them of wealth and children (23:56) We compete for good works for them? Nay! They are not aware. (23:57) Truly those, they who dread their Lord and are ones who are apprehensive (23:58) and those, they who believe in the signs of their Lord (23:59) and those, they who make not partners with their Lord (23:60) and those, they who give what they give with their hearts quaking because they are ones who will return to their Lord (23:61) are those who compete with one another in good works and they are ones who outstrip them.

Chapter 24 The Light 12 Signs

(24:19) Truly those who love that indecency be spread among those who have believed, they will have a painful punishment in the present and in the world to come. And God knows and you know not. (24:20) And had it not been for the grace of God on you and His mercy, you would be ruined for God is Gentle, Compassionate. (24:21) O those who have believed! Follow not in the steps of Satan. And whoever follows in the steps of Satan, then truly he commands depravity, and that which was immoral. And had it not been for the grace of God on you and His mercy, none of you would ever have been pure in heart, but God makes pure whom He wills, and God is Hearing, Knowing. (24:22) And forswear not those with grace and plenty among you to give to kin and the needy and the ones who emigrate in the way of God and let them pardon and let them overlook, love you not that God should forgive you, and God is Forgiving, Compassionate.

(24:51) The only saying of the ones who believe has been - when they were called to God and His Messenger that He give judgment between them—to say: We heard and obeyed. And those, they are the ones who prosper. (24:52) And whoever obeys God and His Messenger and dreads God and is Godfearing, those, they are the ones who are victorious.

Chapter 25 The Criterion 15 Signs

(25:63) And the servants of The Merciful are those who walk on the earth in meekness. And when the ones who are ignorant address them, they say: Peace! (25:64) And those who spend the night with their Lord as ones who prostrate themselves and are upright, (25:65) and those who say: Our Lord! Turn us away from the punishment of hell; truly its punishment has been continuous torment. (25:66) Truly it is evil an habitation and resting place. (25:67) And those who, when they spend, neither exceed all bounds nor are they tightfisted. And there is between those two extremes a just stand: (25:68) Those who call not to another god other than

God nor kill the soul which God has forbidden but rightfully nor commit adultery. And whoever disregards and commits this will meet sinfulness. (25:69) The punishment will be multiplied for him on the Day of Resurrection and he will dwell in it forever as one who is despised. (25:70) But whoever repents and believes and one whose actions act in accord with morality, for those God will substitute for their evil deeds benevolence, and God has been Forgiving, Compassionate. (25:71) And whoever repents and one who acts in accord with morality, he truly repents to God, turning in repentance. (25:72) And those who bear not witness to untruth and if they pass by idle talk, they pass by nobly. (25:73) And those who when they were to be reminded of the signs of their Lord, fall not down unwilling to hear and unwilling to see. (25:74) And those who say: Our Lord! Bestow on us from our wives and our offspring the comfort of our eyes and make us leaders of ones who are Godfearing, (25:75) those will be given recompense in the highest chambers because they patiently endured. They will be in receipt of greetings and peace, (25:76) ones who will dwell in it forever. An excellent habitation and resting place! (25:77) Say: My Lord would not concern Himself with you had it not been for your supplication; but surely you have denied so it will be close at hand.

Chapter 26 The Poets 14 Signs

(26:213) So call not to any god other than God so that thou be among the ones who were punished. (26:214) And warn thy nearest kin, kinspeople. (26:215) And make low thy wing to those who would follow thee among the ones who believe. (26:216) Then if they rebel against thee, then say: Truly I am free of what they do. (26:217) And put thy trust in The Almighty, The Compassionate, (26:218) Who sees thee at the time thou hast stood up (26:219) and thy going to and fro among the ones who prostrate themselves? (26:220) Truly He is The Hearing, The Knowing. (26:221) Will I tell you in whom the devils come forth? (26:222) They come forth in every sinful false one who gives listen, (26:223) but most of them are ones who lie. (26:224) As for the poets, ones who are in error follow them. (26:225) Hast thou not considered that they wander in every valley (26:226) and that they say what they accomplish not? (26:227) But those who have believed and the ones who act in accord with morality remember God frequently and help themselves after wrong was to be done to them, and those who do wrong will soon know by what overturning they will be turned about!

Chapter 27 The Ant 11 Signs

(27:1) Ṭā Sīn. These are the signs of the Quran and a clear Book, (27:2) a guidance and good tidings for the ones who believe, (27:3) those who perform the formal prayer and give the purifying alms so that they, they are certain of the world to come. (27:4) Truly as for those who believe not in the world to come, We have made their actions appear pleasing to them so that they wander unwilling to see. (27:5) Those are they for whom is the tragic punishment and they, in the world to come, they are the ones who are the losers. (27:6) And truly thou be in receipt of the Quran, that which proceeds from the Presence of One who is Wise, Knowing.

(27:89) Whoever draws near with benevolence, for him will be better than it and they would be from the terror ones who are safe on that Day. (27:90) And whoever draws near with evil deeds, they would be slung on their faces in the fire: Are you given recompense but with what you had been doing? (27:91) Truly I was commanded to worship the Lord of this land which He has made sacred and to Whom all things belong; and I was commanded to be of the ones who submit (27:92) and to recount the Quran; so whoever is truly guided, then he is truly guided only for himself; and to whoever goes astray say: Truly I am of the ones who warn. (27:93) And say: The Praise belongs to God. He will cause you to see His signs and you will recognize them. Thy Lord is not One Who is Heedless of what you do.

Chapter 28 The Story 5 Signs

(28:60) And whatever things you were to be given are enjoyment for this present life and its adornment. And what is with God is better for one who endures. Will you not then be reasonable? (28:61) Is he to whom We promised a fair promise—and it is one that reaches fulfillment—like him to whom We have given the enjoyment of enjoyment for this present life? After that on the Day of Resurrection he he will be among the ones who were charged?

(28:77)) Be looking for what God has given thee for the Last Abode; and forget not thy share of the present; and do good even as God has been a doer of good to thee; and be not insolent, corrupting in and on the earth; truly God loves not the ones who make corruption.

(28:83) This is the Last Abode that We will assign to those who want not self-exaltation in the earth nor corruption. And the Ultimate End is for the ones who are Godfearing. (28:84) Whoever brings about benevolence, for him there will be better than it; and whoever brings about an evil deed, then not will be given recompense to those who do evil deeds other than for what they had been doing.

Chapter 29 The Spider 7 Signs

(29:41) The parable of those who take other than God to themselves as protectors is that of the spider who takes a house to itself; but truly the frailest of houses is the house of the spider if they had but known. (29:42) Truly God knows what thing they call to other than Him. And He is The

Almighty, The Wise. (29:43) And We propound these parables for humanity; and no one is reasonable among them but the ones who have knowledge. (29:44) God created the heavens and the earth with The Truth. Truly in that is a sign for the ones who believe. (29:45) Recount what was to be revealed to thee of the Book and perform the formal prayer; truly the formal prayer prohibits greater depravity and that which was immoral, and truly the remembrance of God is greater, and God knows what

(29:56) O my servants who have believed, My earth truly is one that is extensive, so worship Me! (29:57) Every soul will be one who experiences death; after that to Us you will be returned.

Chapter 30 The Romans 5 Signs

(30:30) So set thy face towards a way of life as a monotheist. It is the nature originated by God in which He originated humanity. There is no substituting the creation of God. That is the truth-loving way of life, except most of humanity knows not. (30:31) Be ones who turn in repentance to Him and be Godfearing and perform the formal prayer and be not among the ones who are polytheists,

(30:36) And when We cause humanity to experience mercy, they are glad of it; but when an evil deed lights on them because of what their hands have put forward, lo and behold! They are in despair. (30:37) Have they not considered that God extends the provision for whom He wills and confines it for whom He wills? Truly in that are signs for a folk who believe. (30:38) So give to kin rightfully and to the needy and to the traveler of the way. That is better for those who want the Countenance of God; and those, they are the ones who prosper.

Chapter 31 Luqman 9 Signs

(31:16) O my son! Truly even if it be the weight of a grain

of a mustard seed and though it be in a rock or in the heavens or in or on the earth God will bring it. Truly God is Subtle, Aware. (31:17) O my son! Perform the formal prayer and command that which was moral and prohibit that which was immoral and have patience with whatever lights on thee; truly that is the constancy of affairs. (31:18) And turn not thy cheek away from humanity nor walk through the earth exultantly; truly God loves not any proud boaster. (31:19) And be moderate in thy walking and lower thy voice. Truly the most horrible of all voices is certainly the voice of the donkey.

(31:22) And whoever submits his face to God while he is one who is a doer of good, then surely he has held fast to the most firm handhold, and to God is the Ultimate End of affairs.

(31:33) O humanity! Be Godfearing of your Lord, and dread a Day when one will not give recompense for another: To one to whom a child is born for his child, nor by one who was a child to the one to whom a child was born at all. (31:34) Truly the promise of God is True; so let not this present life delude you nor let the deluder delude you about God. Truly the knowledge of the Hour is with God and He sends plenteous rain water down and He knows what is in the wombs; and no soul is informed of what it will earn tomorrow and no soul is informed in what region it will die. Truly God is Knowing, Aware.

Chapter 32 The Prostration 5 Signs
(32:15) Only those believe in Our signs who, when they were to be reminded of them, fall down, ones who prostrate themselves and glorify the praise of their Lord and they grow not arrogant, (32:16) whose sides deliberately avoid their sleeping places to call to their Lord in fear and hope. And they spend of what We have provided them. (32:17) No

soul knows what was to be concealed for them of comfort for their eyes as a recompense for what they had been doing. (32:18) Is he who has been one who believes like he who has been one who disobeys? They are not on the same level. (32:19) As for those who have believed and the ones who have acted in accord with morality, for them are Gardens as places of shelter, a welcome to them for what they had been doing.

Chapter 33 The Confederates 10 Signs

(33:23) Among the ones who believe are men who are sincere in the contracts they have made with God; of them are some who satisfy by fulfilling their vow with death and of them are some who wait and watch; and they have not substituted any substitution (33:24) so that God may give recompense to the ones who are sincere for their sincerity and punish the ones who are hypocrites had He willed or He turns to them in forgiveness. Truly God has been Forgiving, Compassionate.

(33:35) Truly the ones who are males who submit and the ones who are females who submit and the ones who are males who believe and the ones who are females who believe and the ones who are morally obligated males and the ones who are morally obligated females and the ones who are sincere males and the ones who are sincere females and the ones who are males who remain steadfast and the ones who are females who remain steadfast and the ones who are humble males and the ones who are humble females and the ones who are charitable males and the ones who are charitable females and the ones who are males who fast and the ones who are females who fast and the males who guard their private parts and the females who guard and ones who are males who remember God frequently and ones who are females who remember, God has prepared for them forgiveness and a sublime compensation. (33:36) It would not be for one who is a male believer and one who is a female believe, when God and His Messenger decreed an affair that there should be any choice for them in their affair, and whoever rebels against God and His Messenger, certainly he goes astray, clearly wandering astray.

(33:41) O those who have believed! Remember God with a frequent remembrance (33:42) and glorify Him in the early morning at dawn and at eventide. (33:43) He it is Who gives blessings to you and His angels that He may bring you out of the shadows into the light. And He has been Compassionate to ones who believe (33:44) Their greetings on the Day they will meet Him will be: Peace! And He has prepared for them a generous compensation.

(33:70) O those who have believed! Be Godfearing of God and say an appropriate saying. (33:71) He will make your actions right for you and forgive you your impieties, and whoever obeys God and His Messenger has surely won a triumph, a sublime triumph! (33:72) Truly We presented the trust to the heavens and the earth and the mountains, but they refused to carry it and were apprehensive of it. But the human being carried it; truly he had been wrongdoing, very ignorant.

Chapter 34 Sheba 1 Sign

(34:37) And it is not your wealth nor your children that will bring you near to Us, but he who has believed and one who has acted in accord with morality. As for those, they will have recompense doubled for what they did and they will live in the high chambers as ones who are in safety.

Chapter 35 The Originator 8 Signs

(35:5) O humanity! Truly the promise of God is true; so let not this present life delude you; and let not the deluder delude you about God. (35:6) Truly Satan is an enemy to you so take him to yourselves as an enemy. He calls only his party that they may become among the Companions of the Blaze.

(35:15) O humanity! It is you who are poor in relation to God; and God—He is Sufficient, Worthy of Praise. (35:16) If He wills, He would cause you to be put away and bring a new creation. And that for God is not a great matter. (35:18) And no burdened soul will bear another's load. If one who was weighed down calls for help for his heavy load, nothing of it will be carried for him, even if he be possessor of kinship. Warnest thou only those who dread their Lord in the unseen and performed the formal prayer. And he who purified himself, then only purifies for himself. And to God is the Homecoming.

(35:29) Truly those who recount the Book of God and performed the formal prayer and spent out of what We have provided for them secretly and in public they hope for a trade that will never come to nothing. (35:30) He will surely pay them their account in full as compensation for them and increase them more out of His grace. Truly He is forgiving, Ready to Appreciate.

Chapter 37 The Ones Standing in Rank 8 Signs

(37:99) He said: Truly I am one who goes to my Lord. He will guide me. My Lord! Bestow on me of the ones who are in accord with morality. (37:101) So We gave him the good tidings of a forbearing boy. And when he reached maturity endeavoring with him, he said: O my son! Truly I see while slumbering that I am sacrificing thee. So look on what thou hast considered? He said: O my father! Accomplish whatever thou art commanded; thou shalt find me, if God willed, of the ones who remain steadfast. (37:103) Then when they had both submitted themselves and he had flung him on his brow (37:104) We cried out to him: O Abraham! Thus truly We give recompense to the ones who are doers of good. (37:106) Truly that was certainly the clear trial.

Chapter 38 Sad 6 Signs

(38:26) O David! Truly We have made you a viceregent on the earth so give judgment duly among humanity and follow not your desire for it will cause you to go astray from the way of God. Truly those who go astray from the way of God, for them there is a severe punishment because they forgot the Day of Reckoning. (38:27) And We created not the heaven and the earth and all that is between the two in falsehood. That is the opinion of those who are ungrateful. Then woe to those who disbelieve in the fire! (38:28) Or will We make those who have believed and the ones who have acted in accord with morality like the ones who make corruption in and on the earth or will We make the ones who are Godfearing as the ones who act immorally? (38:29) It is a blessed Book that We have sent forth to thee so that they may meditate on its signs and those who have intuition may recollect.

(38:86) Say: I ask of you not for any compensation for this nor am I among the ones who take things upon themselves. (38:87) It is nothing other than a Remembrance for the worlds (38:88) and you will certainly know its tidings after awhile.

Chapter 39 The Troops 7 Signs

(39:9) Is he one who is morally obligated during the night watch, one who prostrates himself or one who is standing up in prayer being fearful of the world to come and hoping for the mercy of his Lord, say: Are those who know on the same level as those who know not, only those who have intuition recollect. (39:10) Say: O My servants who have believed! Be Godfearing of your Lord. For those who do good in the present, there is benevolence, and the earth of God is extensive; only ones who remain steadfast will have their compensation paid in full without reckoning. (39:11) Say: Truly I was commanded to worship God, one who is sincere and devoted in the way of life to Him. (39:12) And I was to be commanded to be the first of the ones who submit.

(39:23) God has sent down the fairest discourse, a Book, one that is consistent in its often repeated parts of the Quran by which shiver the skins of those who dread their Lord. Their skins and their hearts become gentle with the Remembrance of God. That is the guidance of God. With it He guides whom He wills. And whomever God causes to go astray, there is not for him anyone who guides.

(39:53) Say: O My servants who have exceeded all bounds against themselves despair not of the mercy of God. Truly God forgives all impieties. Truly He is The Forgiving, The Compassionate. (39:54) Be penitent to your Lord and submit to Him before the punishment approaches you. After that you will not be helped. (39:55) And follow the fairest of what was sent forth to you from your Lord before the punishment approaches you suddenly while you are not aware

Chapter 40 The One Who Forgives

(40:39) O my folk! Truly this present life is nothing but transitory enjoyment and that the world to come is the stopping place, the Abode. (40:40) Whoever does an evil deed will not be given recompense but the like of it; but one who has acted in accord with morality, whether male or female, and such is one who believes, then those will enter the Garden where they will be provided in it without reckoning.

Chapter 41 They Were Explained Distinctly 4 Signs

(41:33) And who has a fairer saying than he who has called to God and one who has acted in accord with morality, and has said: I am one of the ones who submit. (41:34) Not on the same level are benevolence or the evil deed. Drive back with what is fairer. Then behold he who between thee and between him was enmity as if he had been a protector, a loyal friend. (41:35) And none will be in receipt of it but those who endure patiently, and none will be in receipt of it but the possessor of a sublime allotment. (41:36) And if a provocation from Satan provokes you, seek refuge in God; truly He is The Hearing, The Knowing.

Chapter 42 The Consultation 9 Signs

(42:20) And they would say: If willed The Merciful, We would not have worshiped them, and they have no knowledge of that; they do nothing but guess.

(42:25) So We requited them; then look on how the Ultimate End had been for the ones who deny. (42:26) Mention when Abraham said to his father and his folk: Truly I am released from obligation to what you worship (42:27) other than Him Who originated me and truly He will guide me.

(42:36) And whoever renders himself weak-sighted to the Remembrance of The Merciful, We allot for him a devil so he is a comrade for him. (42:37) And truly they bar them from the way, but they assume that they are ones who are truly guided. (42:38) Then when he draws near to us he would say: Would that there were a distance between me and between thee of two sunrises! How miserable is the comrade. (42:39) And it will never profit you this Day as you did wrong. You will be ones who are partners in the punishment. (42:40) So wilt thou cause someone unwilling to hear, to hear or wilt thou guide the unwilling to see or someone who has been clearly going astray?

Chapter 43 The Ornaments 5 Signs

(43:32) Would they divide the mercy of thy Lord? It is We

Who divided out among them their livelihood in this present life. Exalted are some of them above some others in degree so that some may take to themselves others in their bondage, and the mercy of thy Lord is better than what they gather. (43:33) And were it not that humanity would have been one community, We would have made for whoever disbelieves in The Merciful, roofs of silver for their houses, and stairways up which they would scale (43:34) and for their houses, doors and couches on which they would recline (43:35) and ornaments? Yet all this would have been nothing but enjoyment of this present life. And the world to come with your Lord is for the ones who are Godfearing. (43:36) And whoever renders himself weak-sighted to the Remembrance of The Merciful, We allot for him a satan so he is a comrade for him.

Chapter 45 The Ones Who Kneel 6 Signs

(45:21) Assumed those who seek to do evil deeds that We will make them equal with those who have believed and the ones who have acted in accord with morality? Are their living and dying equal? Evil is the judgment they give! (45:22) And God created the heavens and the earth with The Truth so that every soul would be given recompense for what it has earned and they will not be done wrong. (45:23) Have you considered him who has taken to himself his own desire as his god and whom God causes to go astray knowingly setting a seal on his having the ability to hear and his heart and laid a blindfold on his sight? Who then will guide him after God? Will you not then recollect?

(45:33) And showing themselves to them will be the evil deeds they have done. They will be surrounded by what they had been ridiculing. (45:34) It would be said: This Day We will forget you as you forgot the meeting of this Day of yours. Your place of shelter will be the fire and there is not for you any one who helps. (45:35) This is because you took the signs of God to yourself in mockery and this present life has deluded you. So this Day they will not be brought out from there nor will they ask to be favored.

Chapter 46 The Curving Sandhills 3 Signs

(46:13) Truly those who say: Our Lord is God and then go straight, neither will there be fear in them, nor will they feel remorse.

(46:35) So have patience as endured patiently those with constancy of the Messengers and let them not seek to hasten the Judgment. As truly on a Day they will see what they are to be promised as if they had not but lingered in expectation but for an hour of daytime. This is delivering the message! Will any be caused to perish but the folk, the ones who disobey?

Chapter 47 Muhammad 6 Signs

(47:24) Meditate they not then on the Quran or are there locks on their hearts? (47:25) Truly those who go back, turning their back after the guidance has become clear to them, it was Satan who enticed them and He granted them indulgence. (47:26) That is because they said to those who disliked what God had sent down: We will obey you in some of the affair; and God knows what they keep secret.

(47:36) This present life is only a pastime and a diversion. But if you believe and are God fearing, He will give you your compensation and will not ask of you for your property. (47:37) If He were to ask it of you and be importunate, you would be a miser and He would bring out your rancor. (47:38) Lo and behold! You are those being called to spend in the way of God, yet among you are some who are miserly; and whoever is miserly, then he is miserly only to himself. God is Sufficient and you are poor. And if you turn away,

He will have a folk other than you in exchange. Then they will not bed the life of you.

Chapter 48 The Victory 2 Signs

(48:28) He it is Who has sent His Messenger with guidance and the way of life of The Truth that He may uplift it over all of the ways of life. And God has sufficed as a witness. (48:29) Muhammad is the Messenger of God. And those who are with him are severe against the ones who are ungrateful, but compassionate among themselves; thou seest them as ones who bow, as ones who prostrate themselves. They are looking for grace from God and contentment; their marks are on their faces from the effects of prostration. This is their parable in the Torah. And their parable in the Gospel is like sown seed that brings out its shoot, then is invigorated. It then becomes stout and rises straight on its plant stalk impressing the ones who are sowers so that He may enrage by them the ones who are ungrateful, God has promised those who have believed and the ones who have acted in accord with morality, for them forgiveness and a sublime compensation.

Chapter 49 The Inner Apartments 6 Signs

(49:12) O those who have believed! Avoid suspicion much. Truly some suspicion is a sin; and spy not nor backbite some by one another. Would one of you love to eat the flesh of his lifeless brother? You would dislike it. And be Godfearing of God. Truly God is Accepter of Repentance, Compassionate. (49:13) O humanity! Truly We have created you from a male and a female and made you into peoples and types that you may recognize one another. Truly the most generous of you with God is the most devout. Truly God is Knowing, Aware.

(49:15) The ones who believe are not but those who have

believed in God and His Messenger. After that they were not in doubt and they struggled with their wealth and themselves in the way of God. Those, they are the ones who are sincere. (49:16) Say: Would you teach God about your way of life while God knows all that is in the heavens and all that is in and on the earth? And God is Knowing of everything. (49:17) They count as a favor to thee that they have submitted; say: Count not as a favor to me your submission; nay! God has done a favor to you in that He has guided you to belief if you truly have been ones who are sincere. (49:18) Truly God knows the unseen of the heavens and the earth. And God is Seeing of what you do.

Chapter 50 Qaf 2 Signs

(50:39) So have patience with whatever they say and glorify with the praise of thy Lord before the coming up of the sun and before sunset (50:40) and in the night glorify Him and at the end part of the prostration.

Chapter 51 The Winnowing Winds 3 Signs

(51:56) And I created not jinn and human kind but that they worship Me. (51:57) I want no provision from them nor want I that they should feed Me. (51:57) Truly God, He is the Provider, the Possessor of Strength, The Sure.

Chapter 52 The Mount 2 Signs

(52:48) So have patience for the determination of thy Lord, for truly thou art under Our eyes; (52:49) and glorify the praises of thy Lord when thou hast stood up at the time of dawn, and glorify at night and the drawing back of the stars.

Chapter 57 Iron 8 Signs

(57:10) And what is the matter with you that you spend

not in the way of God? And to God belongs the heritage of the heavens and the earth? Not on the same level are those among you who spent before the victory and fought. Those are more sublime in degree than those who spent afterwards and fought. And God has promised fairness to all. And God is Aware of what you do.

(57:18) Truly the ones who are males who give in charity and the ones who are females who give in charity and who lend a fair loan to God, it will be multiplied for them and for them there is a generous compensation. (57:19) And those who have believed in God and His Messengers, those, they are the just persons; and the witnesses to their Lord. For them is their compensation and their light; and those who were ungrateful and denied Our signs, those are the Companions of Hellfire. (57:20) Know that this present life is only a pastime, a diversion and an adornment and a mutual boasting among you and a rivalry in respect to wealth and children; as the likeness of plenteous rain water. The vegetation impresses ones who are ungrateful. After that it withers, becoming yellow. After that it becomes chaff; while in the world to come there is severe punishment, and forgiveness from God and contentment. And this present life is nothing but a delusion of enjoyment. (57:21) Race towards forgiveness from your Lord and towards the Garden whose depth is as the breadth of the heavens and earth. It was prepared for those who have believed in God and His Messengers. That is the grace of God. He gives it to whom He wills. And God is The Possessor of the Sublime Grace. (57:22) And no affliction lights on the earth nor on yourselves but it is in a Book that We fashioned before. Truly that is easy for God, (57:23) so that you not grieve over what has passed away from you nor be glad because of what has been given to you, and God loves not any proud, boastful one. (57:24) Those who are misers and who command humanity to miserliness, and whoever turns away then God, He is The Sufficient, The Worthy of Praise.

Chapter 59 The Banishment 2 Signs

(59:18) O those who have believed! Be Godfearing of God and let every person look on what it has put forward for tomorrow; and be Godfearing of God. Truly God is Aware of what you do. (59:19) And be not like those who forgot God and He caused them to forget themselves. Those, they are the ones who disobey. The Companions of the Fire are not equal to the Companions of the Garden. (59:20) The Companions of the Gardens, they are the ones who are victorious.

Chapter 61 The Ranks 2 Signs

(61:10) O those who have believed! Shall I point you to a transaction that will rescue you from a painful punishment? (61:11) You believe in God and His Messenger and struggle in the way of God with your wealth and your lives. That is better for you if you would know.

Chapter 62 The Congregation 4 Signs

(62:8) Say: Truly the death that you run away from, then it will be truly that which you encounter; after that you will be returned to the One Who has Knowledge of the unseen and the visible and He will tell you what you had been doing. (62:9) O those who have believed! When the formal prayer was to be proclaimed on the day of Friday, then hasten to the Remembrance of God and forsake trading. That is better for you if you had been knowing. (62:10) Then when the formal prayer was to end, be you diffused through the earth, looking for the grace of God. And remember God frequently so that perhaps you would prosper. (62:11) And when they consider a transaction or a diversion, they break away toward it, and leave thee as one who is standing. Say: What is with God is better than any diversion or than any transaction. And God is The Best of the ones who provide.

Chapter 63 The Hypocrites 4 Signs

(63:9) O those who have believed! Let not your wealth divert you nor your children from the Remembrance of God. And whoever accomplishes that, then those are the ones who are losers. (63:10) And spend what We have provided you before approaches death to any of you. Then he will say: My Lord! If only Thou wouldst postpone it for a little term then I would be charitable and be among the ones who are in accord with morality. (63:11) But God will never postpone it for a soul when its term has drawn near. And God is Aware of what you do.

Chapter 64 The Mutual Loss and Gain 8 Signs

(64:11) No affliction would light but with the permission of God, whoever believes in God, He guides his heart. And God is Knowing of everything. (64:12) And obey God and obey the Messenger. Then if you turn away, then it is only for Our Messenger delivering the clear message. (64:13) God, there is no god but He. And in God let the ones who believe put their trust. (64:14) O those who have believed! Truly there are among your wives and your children enemies for you, so beware of them. And if you would pardon, overlook and forgive, then truly God is Forgiving, Compassionate. (64:15) Your wealth and your children are only a test. And God, with Him is a sublime compensation. (64:16) So be Godfearing of God as much as you are able and hear and obey and spend. That is good for yourselves, and whoever is protected from his own stinginess, then those, they are the ones who prosper. (64:17) If you lend to God a fair loan, He will multiply it for you and will forgive you. And God is Ready to Appreciate, Forbearing, (64:18) One Who has Knowledge of the unseen and the visible The Almighty, The Wise.

Chapter 65 Divorce 4 Signs

(65:1) O Prophet! When you divorce your wives, then divorce them (f) after their (f) waiting periods and count their (f) waiting periods; and be Godfearing of God, your Lord; and drive them (f) not out from their (f) houses nor let them (f) go forth unless they approach a glaring indecency. These are the ordinances of God. And whoever violates the ordinances of God, then truly he has done wrong to himself. Thou art not informed so that perhaps God would cause to be evoked something after that affair. (65:2) Then when they (f) have reached their (f) term, either hold them (f) back as one who was honorable or part with them (f) as one who was honorable and call to witness two just persons from among you and perform testimony for God. That is admonished with it for whomever has been believing in God and the Last Day. And he who is Godfearing of God, He will make a way out for him. (65:3) And He will provide him from where he not anticipate. And whoever puts his trust in God, then He will be enough for him. God is One Who Carries Through His command. Surely God has assigned a measure to everything. (65:4) And as for those who give up hope of menstruation among your women, if you are in doubt, their (f) waiting period is three months and for those who have not yet menstruated. As for those who are pregnant women, their (f) term is until they bring forth a baby. And whoever is Godfearing of God, He will make his affair easy for him. (65:5) That is the command of God which He has sent forth to you. And whoever is Godfearing of God, He will absolve him of his evil deeds and will enhance for him a compensation.

Chapter 66 The Forbidding 1 Sign

(66:8) O those who have believed! Turn to God for forgiveness remorsefully, faithfully. Perhaps your Lord will absolve you of your evil deeds and cause you to enter into Gardens beneath which rivers run. On the Day God will not cover the Prophet with shame and those who have believed with him; their light will hasten about before them and on their right. They will say: Our Lord! Fulfill for us our light and forgive us; truly Thou art Powerful over all things.

Chapter 70 The Stairways of Ascent 17 Signs

(70:19) Truly the human being was created fretful. (70:20) When the worst afflicts him, he is impatient. (70:21) And when good afflicts him, begrudging, (70:22) but those who are devoted to their formal prayer, (70:23) those who, they are ones who continue with their formal prayers (70:24) and those who in their wealth there is a known obligation towards (70:25) the one who seeks and the one who was an outcast (70:26) and those who sincerely validate the Day of Judgment, (70:27) and those, they who (70:28) are apprehensive of the punishment of their Lord. Truly as to the punishment of their Lord, there is no one who was in security from it. (70:29) Those, they who are ones who guard their private parts (70:30) but from their spouses or what their right hands possess. Truly they are not ones who will be reproached. (70:31) But whoever would look beyond that, those, they are ones who are turning away. (70:32) And those, they who (70:33) in their trusts and to their compacts are ones who shepherd and those, they who their testimony are ones who uphold and those, they are (70:34) watchful of their formal prayers, (70:35) those will be in Gardens, ones who were honored.

Chapter 72 The Jinn 8 Signs

(72:16) If they had gone straight on the way, We would

have given them to satiate themselves of copious water (72:17) so that We try them in it. But whoever turns aside from the Remembrance of his Lord, He will dispatch him to a rigorous punishment. (72:18) Truly the places of prostration belong to God so call not to any other with God. (72:19) And truly when the servant of God stood up, calling on Him, they were about to swarm upon him. (72:20) Say: Truly I call only to my Lord, and I make no one partners with Him. (72:21) Say: Truly I possess not the power to hurt nor to bring right mindedness for you. (72:22) Say: Truly never would grant me protection from God anyone; and never will I find other than Him that which was a haven (72:23) unless I truthfully deliver what I receive from God and His messages. And whoever disobeys God and His Messenger, then for him is the fire of hell, ones who will dwell in it forever, eternally.

Chapter 73 The One Who is Wrapped 10 Signs

(73:1) O thou, the one who is wrapped, (73:2) stand up during the night, but for a little part, (73:3) for half of it or reduce it a little. (73:4) Or increase it and chant the Quran, a good chanting, (73:5) for We will cast on thee a weighty saying. (73:6) Truly one should begin in the nighttime when impression is more vigorous and speech more upright. (73:7) Truly for thee in the daytime is a lengthy occupation. (73:8) And remember the Name of thy Lord. And devote thyself to Him with total devotion. (73:9) The Lord of the East and of the West, there is no god but He. So take Him to thyself as thy Trustee. (73:10) And have patience with regard to what they say and abandon them with a sweet abandonment.

Chapter 74 The One Who is Wrapped in a Cloak 7 Signs

(74:1) O thou, the one who has wrapped himself in a cloak! (74:2) Stand up and warn! (74:3) And magnify thy

Lord (74:4) and purify thy garments (74:5) and abandon defilement! (74:6) And show grace not to acquire more. (74:7) And for thy Lord, then have patience.

Chapter 76 The Human Being 7 Signs

(76:23) Truly We have sent down to thee the Quran, a sending down successively. (76:24) So have thou patience for the determination of thy Lord and obey not any one of them, not the ones who are perverted nor the ungrateful. (76:25) And remember thou the Name of thy Lord in the early morning and in the eventide. (76:26) And during the night, prostrate thyself to Him and glorify Him a lengthy part of the night. (76:27) Truly these, they love that which hastens away and they forsake a weighty day behind them. (76:28) We have created them and We strengthened their frame; and when We willed, We will substitute their likes as a substitution. (76:29) Truly this is an admonition; and whoever willed, he may take a way to his Lord. (76:30) But you will it not unless God wills it. For God has been Knowing, Wise. (76:31) He causes to enter whom He wills into His mercy. And the ones who are unjust, He has made ready for them a painful punishment.

Chapter 79 The Ones Who Tear Out 7 Signs

(79:35) on that Day the human being will recollect for what he endeavored. (79:36) Hellfire was to be advanced for whoever sees. (79:37) As for whoever was defiant (79:38) and held this present life in greater favor, (79:39) then truly hellfire was to be the place of shelter! (79:40) And as for him who feared the Station of his Lord and prohibited desire from his soul, (79:41) truly the Garden will be the place of shelter!

Chapter 84 The Splitting Open 4 Signs

(84:6) O human being! Truly thou art one who is laboring

toward thy Lord laboriously and thou wilt be one who encounters Him. (84:7) And as for him who was to be given his
book in his right hand, (84:8) then he will be reckoned an
easy reckoning, (84:9) and who will turn about to his people
as one who is gladdened.

Chapter 87 The Lofty 6 Signs

(87:14) He certainly prospered, he who purified himself,
(87:15) and remembered the Name of his Lord and invoked
blessings. (87:16) Nay! You hold this present life in greater
favor, (87:17) yet the world to come is better, and one that
endures. (87:18) Truly this is in the previous scrolls, (87:19)
the scrolls of Abraham and Moses.

Chapter 89 The Dawn 6 Signs

(89:15) Then as for the human being, when his Lord tests
hi and honors him and lauds him, he says: My Lord honors
me. (89:16) But whenever He tests him and constricts his
provision for him, he says: My Lord despises me. (89:17) No
indeed; nay! You honor not the orphan (89:18) and you encourage not one another about food for the needy (89:19) and
you consume the inheritance, a greedy eating, (89:20) and
you cherish wealth with an ardent love.

Chapter 90 The Land 10 Signs

(90:11) Yet he has not rushed onto the steep ascent.
(90:12) What will cause thee to recognize what the steep ascent is? (90:13) It is the liberating of a bondsperson (90:14) or
feeding on a day of famine (90:15) an orphan near of kin
(90:16) or a needy in misery. (90:17) After that it is among
those who have believed and counseled one another to patience and counseled one another to clemency. (90:18) Those
will be the Companions of the Right Hand. (90:19 But they
who were ungrateful for Our signs they will be the Compan-

ions of the Left Hand (90:20) and over them fire will be a cover.

Chapter 91 The Sun 4 Signs

(91:7) and by the soul and what shaped it (91:8) and then inspired it to its acting immorally and God-consciousness. (91:9) He who makes it pure prospers (91:10) surely is frustrated whoever seduces it.

Chapter 92 The Night 11 Signs

(92:4) truly your endeavors are to diverse ends. (92:5) As for him who gave and is Godfearing (92:6) and established the fair as true, (92:7) We will make easy for him the easing. (92:8) And as for him who was a miser and was self-sufficient (92:9) and denied the fair, (92:10) We will make falling into difficulty easy for him. (92:11) And his wealth will not avail him when he has passed. (92:12) Truly guidance is from Us (92:13) and truly to Us belongs the last and the first. (92:14) I have warned you of a fire that blazes fiercely.

Chapter 93 The Forenoon 3 Signs

(93:9) So as for the orphan, oppress him not. (93:10) And as for one who seeks, scold him not. (93:11) And as for the divine blessing of thy Lord, divulge it!

Chapter 96 The Blood Clot 7 Signs

(96:1) Rubies and Pearls: Recite in the Name of thy Lord Who created. (96:2) He created the human being from a clot. (96:3) Recite: Thy Lord is the Most Generous, (96:4) He Who taught by the pen. (96:5) He taught the human being what he knows not. (96:6) No indeed! The human being is truly defiant. (96:7) He considers himself to be one who is self-sufficient. (96:8) Truly to thy Lord is the return.

Chapter 99 The Convulsion 2 Signs

(99:7) And whoever does the weight of an atom of good will see it. (99:8) And whoever does the weight of an atom of the worst will see it.

Chapter 100 The Chargers 6 Signs

(100:6) Truly the human being is unthankful to his Lord. (100:7) And truly he is a witness to that. (100:8) And he is more severe in the cherishing of good. (100:9) Knows he not that when all that is in the graves was to be scattered (100:10) and was to be shown forth what is hidden in the breasts (100:11) truly their Lord on that Day will be Aware of them.

Chapter 102 The Rivalry 8 Signs

(102:1) Rivalry diverts you (102:2) until you have stopped by the cemetery. (102:3) No indeed! Soon you will know! (102:4) Again, no indeed! You will know! (102:5) No indeed! Soon you will know with the knowledge of certainty. (102:6) You would certainly see hellfire. (102:7) After that you would see it with the eye of certainty. (102:8) After that you will certainly be asked on that day about the bliss.

Chapter 103 By Time 3 Signs

(103:1) By time through the ages, (103:2) truly the human being is surely in a loss (103:3) but those who have believed and the ones who have acted in accord with morality, and have counseled one another to The Truth, and have counseled each other to endure patiently.

Chapter 104 The Slanderer 3 Signs

(104:1) Woe to every slandering backbiter (104:2) who has gathered wealth and counts it over and over! (104:3) He assumes that his wealth has made him immortal.

Chapter 107 Assistance 7 Signs

(107:1) Hast thou considered one who denies this way of life? (107:2) And that is he who drives away with force the orphan (107:3) and urges not to give food to the needy. (107:4) So woe to ones who formally pray, (107:5) ones who are inattentive to their formal prayers, (107:6) those who show off, (107:7) yet they repulse giving the assistance.

Chapter 110 The Help 3 Signs

(110:1) When the help of God draws near and the victory (110:2) and thou hast seen humanity entering into the way of life of God in units, (110:3) then glorify the praise of thy Lord and ask for His forgiveness. Truly He has been ever The Accepter of Repentance.

Chapter 113 The Daybreak 5 Signs

(113:1) Say: I take refuge with the Lord of Daybreak (113:2) from the worst of those things which He has created. (113:3) And from the worst of the darkening of the night when it intensifies. (113:4) And from the worst of the women who blow on the knots. (113:5) And from the worst of one who is jealous when he is jealous.

Chapter 114 Humanity 6 Signs

(114:1) Say: I take refuge with the Lord of the humanity, (114:2) The King of humanity, (114:3) The God of humanity, (114:4) from the worst of the sneaking whisperer of evil (114:5) who whispers evil in the breasts of humanity, (114:6) from among the genie and humanity.

Part 4: Conclusion

Know that we have limited ourselves to classifying the Quranic signs into Rubies and Pearls for two reasons. The first is that the rest of the signs of the Quran are too many to be listed. The second reason is that these are the most important two classes of signs of the Quran.

The basis of faith is knowledge of God. Following this knowledge comes journeying on the straight path back to God. In regard to the world to come, for instance, it is sufficient to have a general belief in it. Whoever knows God and obeys God will certainly be returned to God to a place of happiness. Whoever denies God or disobeys God will certainly be returned to God to a place of misery. To have knowledge of this is not a criterion for undertaking the journey back to Him. Knowledge of this, however, does help increase one's yearning for happiness and acts as a warning against the return to a place of misery.

It may also be that some signs contain both rubies and pearls. We have not indicated them unless the two groups are predominate. It is important that you continue to reflect on these two types of signs because it is this knowledge from which you will attain the greatest happiness.

May God have you and us be among those made most happy because of His mercy, generosity, strength and compassion. Certainly God is The Generous, The Compassionate, The Merciful.

ALCHEMY OF HAPPINESS 2 Vol. set. Abu Hamid al-Ghazzali (A). Jay R. Crook (T), pp. 1260. Chicago: Kazi Publications. The first complete English translation of *The Alchemy of Happiness*, this is Imam Ghazzali's own Persian summary of his famous Arabic treatise on morality and ethics in Islam, *The Revival of Religious Sciences*. In this work, Ghazzali details the many pitfalls, snares, and distractions—internal and external—that lie in wait to divert the traveler of the Way from attaining the goal which Ghazzali calls "spiritual happiness." But there are also defenders, guides, and helpers which the traveler may enlist in his aid if he recognizes them. In *The Alchemy*, Ghazzali has provided the traveler of the Way with a critique of faith and a detailed guidebook to guide him safely to that goal. If he follows its counsels, he will successfully pass through the awesome tribunal of the Resurrection to achieve everlasting salvation, the highest degree of which is that state in which there remains neither fear of the terrors of hell nor appetite for the pleasures of Paradise. It is the pure ecstasy of the loving Divine Presence: Absolute spiritual happiness.

AL-GHAZZALI ALCHEMY OF HAPPINESS ABRIDGED. Claude Field (T). pp. 64, a short summary of Imam Ghazzali's 1300 page work.

AL-GHAZZALI BOOK OF KNOWLEDGE. Abu Hamid Muhammad al- Ghazzali (A). Nabih Amin Faris (T) pp. 240, a translation of a part of al-Ghazzali's famous *Ihya ulum al-Din* called *Kitab al-ilm* or The Book of Knowledge.

AL-GHAZZALI CONFESSIONS. Abu Hamid Muhammad al- Ghazzali (A). Claud Field (T). pp. 70. Translated into English for the first time, this short work gives insight into al-Ghazzali's mind and his decision to come to "know self."

AL-GHAZZALI DELIVERANCE FROM ERROR AND OTHER WORKS. Abu Hamid Muhammad Ghazzali (A). R. J. McCarthy (T), contains five works of al-Ghazzali: 1) *Deliverance from Error (al-Munqidh min aldalal)*; 2) *Explanation of the Wonders of the Heart (Kitab sharh ajaib al-qalb)*; 3) *Correct Balance (al-Qistas al-mustaqim)*; 4) *Noblest Aims in the Explanation of God's Fairest Names (al-Maqsad al-asna fi sharh maani asma Allah al-Husna)*; 5) *Clear Criterion for Distinguishing Between Islam and Godlessness (Faysal al-tafriqa bayn al-islam wa 'l-zandaqa)*; 6) *The Injuries of the Batinites and Virtues of the Mustazhietes (Fadih al-batiniyya wa fadail al-mustazhiriyya)*.

AL-GHAZZALI DUTIES OF BROTHERHOOD IN ISLAM. Abu Hamid

Muhammad al- Ghazzali (A). Muhtar Holland (T). pp. 95, an English translation of a part of the famous work by al-Ghazali, Ihya ulum al-Din.

AL-GHAZZALI FAITH IN DIVINE UNITY AND TRUST IN DIVINE PROVIDENCE. Abu Hamid Muhammad al-Ghazzali (A). David Burrell (T) pp. 180.

Ghazzali's judicious use of stories is intended to imitate the Sufi practice of masterkdisciple, where the novice is helped to discern how to act. The challenge of understanding the relation of the free creator to the universe becomes the task of rightly responding to events as they happen in such a way that the true ordering of things, the divine decree, can be made manifest in our actions-asresponses. When put into practice in this way, the knowledge which faith in divine unity brings can lead us to an habitual capacity (state) to align our otherwise errant responses to situation after situation according to our faith.

AL-GHAZZALI FOUNDATIONS OF THE ARTICLES OF FAITH. Abu Hamid Muhammad al- Ghazzali (A). Nabih Amin Faris (T). pp. 144, a translation of a part of al-Ghazzali's famous *Ihya ulum al-Din* called *"Kitab qawaid al-aqaid."*

AL-GHAZZALI IHYA ULUM AL-DIN, VOLS. I-IV. Abu Hamid Muhammad al- Ghazzali (A). Fazul-ul- Karim (T). pp. 1000, an abridged translation of the famous work of al-Ghazali, *Revival of the Religious Sciences.*

AL-GHAZZALI INCOHERENCE OF THE PHILOSOPHERS. Abu Hamid al- Ghazzali (A). pp. 580, a new translation of this classic work by al-Ghazzali, *Tahafut al-falasifah*, in which al- Ghazzali shows how philosophers err as opposed to theologians.

AL-GHAZZALI INNER DIMENSIONS OF ISLAMIC WORSHIP. Abu Hamid Muhammad al- Ghazzali (A). Muhtar Holland (T). pp. 142, a translation of a selection from al-Ghazzali's famous *Ihya ulum al-Din.*

AL-GHAZZALI INVOCATIONS AND SUPPLICATIONS. Abu Hamid Muhammad al- Ghazzali (A). K. Nakamura (T). pp. 132, a translation of *Kitab al-adhkar wa'l daawat* from the *Ihya ulum al-din.*

AL-GHAZZALI JEWELS OF THE QURAN. Abu Hamid Muhammad al-Ghazzali (A). Laleh Bakhtiar (E). pp. 200, a translation of Imam Ghazzali's *Jawahir al- quran.* In the first part, Imam Ghazzali describes the way to understand the Quran, its principal aims and how all branches of Islamic knowledge are based on it. The second part contains more than 1500 verses from the Quran which Imam Ghazzali divides into rubies and pearls. The signs he describes as rubies relate to our cognitive function and refer to the essence of God, his names and qualities and acts. The signs he describes as pearls refer us to the straight path and the divine urging us to follow it. The pearls engage our practical function.

AL-GHAZZALI JUST BALANCE. Abu Hamid Muhammad al- Ghazzali (A). D. P. Brewster (T). pp. 142, a translation of al-Ghazzali's *al-Qistas al-mustaqim*.

AL-GHAZZALI MISHKAT AL-ANWAR. Abu Hamid Muhammad al-Ghazzali (A). W. H. Gardner (T). pp. 175, a complete translation of al-Ghazzali's famous *Niche of Lights*.

AL-GHAZZALI MYSTERIES OF ALMSGIVING. Abu Hamid Muhammad al- Ghazzali (A). Nabih Amin Faris (T). pp. 98, a translation of a part of al-Ghazzali's famous *Ihya ulum al-Din (Revival of the Religious Sciences)*.

AL-GHAZZALI MYSTERIES OF FASTING. Abu Hamid Muhammad al- Ghazzali (A). Nabih Amin Faris (T). pp. 64, a translation of a part of al-Ghazzali's famous *Ihya ulum al-Din (Revival of the Religious Sciences)*.

AL-GHAZZALI MYSTERIES OF PURITY. Abu Hamid Muhammad al- Ghazzali (A). Nabih Amin Faris (T). pp. 80, a translation of a part of al-Ghazzali's famous *Ihya ulum al-Din (Revival of the Religious Sciences)*.

AL-GHAZZALI MYSTERIES OF THE HUMAN SOUL. Abu Hamid Muhammad al- Ghazzali (A). Abdul Qayyum Hazarvi (T). pp. 64, a translation of a part of al-Ghazzali's *al-Madnun bihi ala ghair ahlihi*.

AL-GHAZZALI MYSTERIES OF WORSHIP IN ISLAM. Abu Hamid Muhammad al- Ghazzali (A). Edwin Elliot Calverley (T). pp. 170, a translation of a part of al-Ghazzali's famous *Ihya ulum al-Din*.

AL-GHAZZALI NINETY-NINE BEAUTIFUL NAMES OF GOD. Abu Hamid Muhammad al- Ghazzali (A). David B. Burrell (T). pp. 205, a complete translation of *al-Maqsad al-asma fi sharh asma Allah al-husna*.

AL-GHAZZALI ON DISCIPLINING THE SELF. Abu Hamid Muhammad al- Ghazzali (A). Muhammad Nur Abdus-Salam (T) pp. 64. Al-Ghazzali places great emphasis on the virtue and spiritual reward of having a good disposition. He also discusses how to recognize the sicknesses of the spiritual heart, the signs of a good character, the raising and training of children, and the prerequisites of becoming a disciple.

This is Bok XXI of Part Three of *The Alchemy of Happiness* entitled The Destroyers.

AL-GHAZZALI ON DISCIPLINING THE SOUL AND ON BREAKING THE TWO DESIRES. Abu Hamid Muhammad al- Ghazzali (A). T. J. Winter (T). pp. 280, a translation from al-Ghazzali's *Revival of Religious Sciences.*

AL-GHAZZALI ON ENJOYING GOOD AND FORBIDDING WRONG Muhammad al- Ghazzali (A). Muhammad Nur Abdus-Salam (T). pp. 32. Al-Ghazzali addresses the necessity of enjoying good (*amr al-maruf*) and forbidding wrongs (*nahy an al-munkar*), the conditions of safeguarding public morality, the fear of the consequences that may occur to oneself from trying to safeguard public morality, the rules of conduct for the guardian of public morality and objectionable acts that are common in custom. This selection is Book XIX of Part Two of *The Alchemy of Happiness* entitled On Mutual Relations.

AL-GHAZZALI ON HOPE AND FEAR Muhammad al- Ghazzali (A) Muhammad Nur Abdus-Salam (T) pp. 64. What is the true nature of hope and how does one attain this virtue? Al-Ghazzali describes the virtue in detail as well as the true nature of fear, the degrees of fear, kinds of fear and the way to acquire fear of God. He relates many stores of messengers and angels, companions and their forefathers. He then asks: which is superior? Hope or fear? This is Book XXXIII of Part Four of *The Alchemy of Happiness* entitled The Deliverers.

AL-GHAZZALI ON KNOWING THIS WORLD AND THE HEREAFTER Muhammad al- Ghazzali (A) Muhammad Nur Abdus-Salam (T) pp. 64, the third and fourth topic of the Introduction of al-Ghazzali to his materful work *The Alchemy of Happiness.* In addition to knowing yourself and God, you need to have some idea about this world and the Hereafter. According to al- Ghazzali, without an understanding of the passing nature of this world and the performance of the Herefater, you may operate out of a different set of values than the ones with which the Creator blessed you.

AL-GHAZZALI ON KNOWING YOURSELF AND GOD Muhammad al- Ghazzali (A) Muhammad Nur Abdus-Salam (T) pp. 64. Al-Ghazzali begins his masterful *The Alchemy of Happiness* with this topic based on the famous Tradition of the Prophet (ص) "One who knows one's self knows one's Lord". In al-Ghazzali's view, everything begins by knowing who you are. He says that you should know that you are born with an outer form and an inner essence or the spiritual heart that you have to come to know in order to know who you are.

AL-GHAZZALI ON LISTENING TO MUSIC Muhammad al- Ghazzali (A) Muhammad Nur Abdus-Salam (T) pp. 32. Al-Ghazzali discusses the difficult issues involved in listening to music and attaining ecstasy through topics like what id unlawful and what is lawful, where listening to music is unlawful, the effects of music and its rules of conduct and the rules of conduct of the whirling dance (sama). This is Book XVIII of Part Two of *The Alchemy of Happiness* entitled On Mutual Relations.

AL-GHAZZALI ON LOVE, LONGING AND CONTENTMENT Muhamamd al- Ghazzali (A) Muhammad Nur Abdus-Salam (T) pp. 64. Al-Ghazzali describes the virtue of love of God and its true nature along with the reasons of love. He explains what longing is, its true nature and how teh eye of the Hereafter is not like the eye of this world. He discusses contentment and uses it as a remedy for achieving love, the signs of love and the virtue and true nature of contentment. This is Book XXXIX of Part Four of *The Alchemy of Happiness* entitled The Deliverers.

AL-GHAZZALI ON MARRIAGE Muhammad al- Ghazzali (A) Muhammad Nur Abdus-Salam (T) pp. 32. In Book XII of Part Two of *The Alchemy of Happiness* entitled On Mutual Relations, al-Ghazzali discusses the benefits and harms of marriage, the manner of contract and its rules, the qualities a man should look for in a wife and the qualities a wife should look for in a husband among other topics.

AL-GHAZZALI ON PATIENCE AND GRATITUDE Muhammad al- Ghazzali (A) Muhammad Nur Abdus-Salam (T) pp. 64. Al-Ghazzali discusses the virtues of patience and gratitude in great detail using examples from the Quran and the Traditions (*ahadith*). Patience is considered to be half of faith and is necessary at all times in all situations according to al-Ghazzali. He explains how one can gain patience. In regard to the virtue of gratitude, he explores its opposite of ingratitude, the true nature of blessings, how knowledge is good and ignorance is evil and blessings and their various degrees. This is Book XXXII of Part Four of *The Alchemy of Happiness* entitled The Deliverers.

AL-GHAZZALI ON RECKONING AND GUARDING Muhammad al- Ghazzali (A) Muhammad Nur Abdus-Salam (T) pp. 32. In this work, al-Ghazzali discusses vigilance and reckoning one's accounts with oneself. He induces a discussion of the vigilance of the truly righteous and how one punishes oneself as well as how one struggles or strives. Emphasis is placed on reproaching or reprimanding the self, a cognitive approach to moral healing. This is Book XXXVI of Part Four of *The Alchemy of Happiness* entitled The Deliverers.

AL-GHAZZALI ON REPENTANCE Muhammad al- Ghazzali (A) Muhammad Nur Abdus-Salam (T) pp. 32. What is the virtue of repentance and its spiritual reward? Al-Ghazali discusses the true nature of repentance, how repentance is a religious duty, how God accepts repentance, minor and major sins, how minor sins become major ones, the prerequisites of repentance, eight acts which atone for sins, the treatment for not being able to repent and whether repentance of certain sins is correct or not. This is Book XXXI of Part Four of *The Alchemy of Happiiness* entitles The Deliverers.

AL-GHAZZALI ON THE DUTIES OF BROTHERHOOD Muhammad al-Ghazzali (A) Muhammad Nur Abdus-Salam (T) pp. 64 For al-Ghazzali, the duties of friendship and brotherhood in association with people include that friendship be for the sake of true love of God Most High. He describes enimity for the sake of God Most High and the degrees of anger against the opponents of God Most High. He also discusses the rights and conditions of association and friendship and the rights of Muslims, neighbors, relatives, mothers and fathers, children and captives in war. This selection is Book XV of Part Two of *The Alchemy of Happiness.*

AL-GHAZZALI ON THE LAWFUL, THE UNLAWFUL AND THE DOUBTFUL Muhammad al- Ghazzali (A) Muhammad Nur Abdus-Salam (T) pp. 32. Al-Ghazzali addresses the spiritual reward and virtue of seeking the lawful, the degrees of the lawful and the unlawful, the seperation of the lawful from the unlawful, stipends given by rulers, and the relations with rulers and teh officials of teh rulers. This selection is Book XIV of Part Two of *The Alchemy of Happiness* entitled On Mutual Relations.

AL-GHAZZALI ON THE MANNERS RELATING TO EATING Abu Hamid Muhammad Ghazzali (A) Denys Johnson-Davies (T) pp. 90. The 11th chapter of the *Ihya Ulum al-Din* begins the section dealing with man and society. The author discusses the habits of eating and finally expounds the virtues of hospitality and generosity and the conduct of the host as well as that of the guest.

AL-GHAZZALI ON THE TREATMENT OF ANGER, HATRED AND ENVY Muhammad al- Ghazzali (A) Muhammad Nur Abdus-Salam (T) pp. 32. Al-Ghazzali discusses the roots of anger that will never be uprooted but how te triumph of God's Unity conceals anger, how the treatment of anger is obligatory along with the causes of anger. In addition he describes hatred and envy, the harms of envy, its true nature, the treatment for envy and how envy must be uprooted from our hearts. This is Book XXIV of Part Three of *The Alchemy of Happiness* entitled The Destroyers.

AL-GHAZZALI ON THE TREATMENT OF HYPOCRISY Muhammad al- Ghazzali (A) Muhammad Nur Abdus-Salam (T) pp. 64. Acts by which people willfully decieve are introduced by al-Ghazzali along with the degrees of hypocrisy, a discussion of hidden hypocrisy, the type of hypocrisy which nullifies good deeds, and the treatment of a spiritual heart sick with the disease of hypocrisy. He then describes acts of devotion which are permitted to be revealed, the sins which are permitted to be concealed and the permission to in some cases refrain from charitable acts out of fear of hypocrisy. This is Book XXVIII of Part Three of *The Alchemy of Happiness* entitled The Destroyers.

AL-GHAZZALI ON THE TREATMENT OF IGNORANCE ARISING FROM HEEDLESSNESS, ERROR AND DELUSION Muhammad al-Ghazzali (A) Muhammad Nur Abdus-Salam (T) pp. 32. Ignorance produces heedlessness, error and delusion according to al-Ghazali. He deals with teh treatment of heedlessness, error and self-delusion or vanity. This is Book XXX of Part Three of *The Alchemy of Happiness* entitled The Destroyers.

AL-GHAZZALI ON THE TREATMENT OF LOVE FOR THIS WORLD Muhammad al- Ghazzali (A) Muhammad Nur Abdus-Salam (T) pp. 32. Al-Ghazzali speaks of the harm of love for this world in the Traditions and then describes the true baseness of this world. This is Book XXV of Part Two of *The Alchemy of Happiness* entitled The Destroyers.

AL-GHAZZALI ON THE TREATMENT OF LOVE OF POWER AND CONTROL Muhammad al- Ghazzali (A) Muhammad Nur Abdus-Salam (T) pp. 32

The treatment of the love of power and control according to al-Ghazzali involves first understanding the true nature of the love and then treating it. He also discusses the treatment for the love of being praised and the different degrees of people concerning praise and blame. This is Book XXVII of Part Three of *The Alchemy of Happiness* entitled The Destroyers.

AL-GHAZZALI ON THE TREATMENT OF MISERLINESS AND

GREED Muhammad al- Ghazzali (A) Muhammad Nur Abdus-Salam (T) pp. 64. Al-Ghazzali speaks on the repugnance of love for wealth as well as when having wealth is praiseworthy, the harm of covetousness and greed and the benefit of contentment, the virtue and spiritual reward of generosity, the blameworthiness of miserliness, the spiritual reward of altruism, the definitions of generosity and miserliness and the enchantment of wealth. This is Book XXVI of Part Three of *The Alchemy of Happiness* entitled The Destroyers.

AL-GHAZZALI ON THE TREATMENT OF PRIDE AND CONCEIT Muhammad al- Ghazzali (A) Muhammad Nur Abdus-Salam (T) pp. 64. The treatment of pride and conceit according to al- Ghazzali is to develop the virtue of humility. He speaks of the nature of pride and its harm, the degrees of pride, and the causes of pride and their treatment in addition to conceit and its harms and the treatment of the moral sickness of conceit. This is Book XXIX of Part Three of *The Alchemy of Happiness* entitled The Destroyers.

AL-GHAZZALI ON THE TREATMENT OF THE HARMS OF THE TONGUE Muhammad al- Ghazzali (A) Muhammad Nur Abdus-Salam (T) pp. 64. Al-Ghazzali speaks out against the harms of tongue like lying and backbiting or maliciously damaging another's reputation as destroyers of one's achieving a good disposition. He also speaks on the spiritual reward of silence and what to do when one is praised. This is Book XXIII of Part Three of *The Alchemy of Happiness* entitled The Destroyers.

AL-GHAZZALI ON TREATMENT OF THE LUST OF THE STOMACH AND THE SEXUAL ORGANS Muhammad al- Ghazzali (A) Muhammad Nur Abdus-Salam (T) pp. 32. Al-Ghazzali discusses the obstacles on the path of faith by offering methods of treatment of the lust of the stomach and the sexual organs as well as the inner mystery of the greater struggle, the harm of checking lust and describing the harms of the lust of sexual organs. This is Book XXII of Part Three of *The Alchemy of Happiness* entitled The Destroyers.

AL-GHAZZALI ON TRUST AND THE UNITY OF GOD Muhammad al- Ghazzali (A) Muhammad Nur Abdus-Salam (T) pp. 64 What is the virtue of trust and the true nature upon which trust is built? What are the degrees of trust and the acts of trust? How does one earn and acquire benefit? How does one repel a loss that has not yet occurred or one that has occurred? What is the remedy for lack of trust in God? Al-Ghazzali addresses these questions and many more in this work. This is Book XXXVIII of Part Four of *The Alchemy of Happiness* entitled The Deliverers.

AL-GHAZZALI ON TRUTHFULNESS AND SINCERITY Muhammad al- Ghazzali (A) Muhammad Nur Abdus-Salam (T) pp. 64. Al-Ghazzali describes the concept of intention in great detail, its true nature and how the intention of the believer is better than his deed. He explores whisperings of the self, evil inspiration and bad thoughts and then those deeds that change according to intention and how admirable servant does what he does for the sake of God. In regard to sincerity, he describes its true nature and then goes on to describe truthfulness. This is Book XXV of Part Four of *The Alchemy of Happiness* entitled The Deliverers.

AL-GHAZZALI PROPER CONDUCT OF MARRIAGE IN ISLAM Imam al- Ghazzali (A) Muhtar Holland (T) pp. 95, a translation of book twelve of the *Ihya Ulum al- Din*.

AL-GHAZZALI RECITATION OF THE QURAN al-Ghazzali Imam Muhammad (A) Laleh Bakhtiar (E) pp. 120. In this translation of a part of Imam Ghazzali's *Ihya ulum al-din* he writes about the purpose of the recitation of the Quran, the external and internal rules of recitation, why it may not be correctly understood and interpretation according to one's own opinion.

AL-GHAZZALI REMEMBRANCE OF DEATH AND THE AFTERLIFE Muhammad al- Ghazzali (A) T. J. Winter (T) pp. 350. This is a translation of *Kitab dhikr al-mawt wa-ma badahu* from the *Ihya ulum al-din*.

LaVergne, TN USA
26 May 2010
184028LV00003B/34/P

9 781567 447606